Retiring to

British Columbia

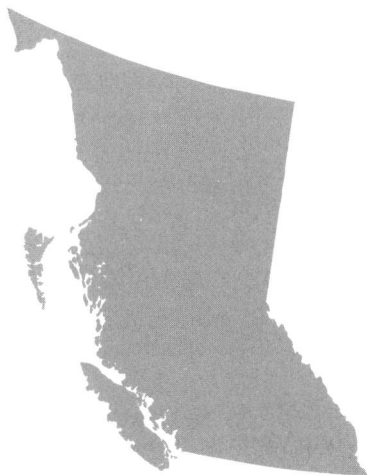

Facts and figures for retiring in British Columbia, plus the story that statistics don't tell.

Newport Bay Publishing • Victoria, B.C.

Contributors: Eric Denhoff
Mark Krasnick
Maury Gwynn
Don Lindenberg
Lon Wood
Carmen Farrell
Tony Kant
Geoff Gwynn

Wills Financial pieces
Mark Horne, of Horne, Coupar,
Manson and Shaw, Victoria

First Edition
September, 1986

Published by Newport Bay Publishing
205 - 560 Johnson Street
Victoria, B.C.
V8W 3C6

International Standard Book Number 0-921513-00-3

Table of Contents

Retirement

For many people who have moved to B.C.'s prime retirement areas, the decision was the right one - an opportunity to golf year-round, enjoy the beauty and majesty of B.C.'s forests, mountains, lakes and ocean, a place to live and enjoy life to its fullest, without long bitter winters. If those things appeal to you, there is something here in B.C. for you.

But for others, the decision to leave family and friends, familiar places and lifelong attachments has been an unhappy experience. Retiring to British Columbia simply isn't for everyone.

Before you decide to make a retirement move, you'll want to take stock of some of those intangibles of your life that will be affected. Can you leave behind the community and circle of friends you now have? How easily do you make new friends? How will a long-distance move affect your relationship with your children and grandchildren?

This book cannot help you wrestle with those questions, but we think it is important that you do deal with them. This book is intended to help you focus on some of the more practical issues involved in retiring to British Columbia, to put some of the romantic, scenic and fantasyland views in perspective.

For example, you will want to know how much it would cost you to live in B.C., which community in B.C. has the most to offer you and what the climate is like.

You must decide whether you want to go on living in a house or whether you seek less responsibility in a condominium or apartment where cutting lawns, weeding gardens and general maintenance are taken care of by someone else.

You may decide to live in a city. Or just outside a city but with easy access to the amenities a city provides. The peace and quiet of the country life may be what you desire.

There are medical considerations which must not be ignored. Availability of a doctor, dentist, hospital and other medical necessities are important factors, as are recreation and entertainment designed to meet your needs and interests.

The ideal situation, of course, is to find one place that provides the right answers to all of those questions. But what attracts one person to a community may be a source of irritation for another person. If Shangri-La exists, it is only in the eye of the beholder.

Our aim here is to highlight six areas for retirement in the province. British Columbia has become the chosen retirement location of tens of thousands of Canadians, and with good reason. Its southwestern corner, including Vancouver and the Lower Mainland, the Okanagan Valley and Vancouver Island, provide temperate weather year-round, acceptable living costs and personal services equal to any found in Canada.

This book focuses on what are known to be the most popular retirement locations in B.C. It is a critical assessment on your behalf, intended to provide the information you need to decide if a community is right for you in your retirement years. If we have done our job well, this book may also prevent you from making a costly mistake.

Throughout the book, you will find the addresses of newspapers and local real estate publications. They are important windows on the community that appeals to you. We urge you to write for subscriptions before moving. It is an excellent way to get a preview of your chosen community.

Southern British Columbia can make no claim to being paradise on earth. Like any other part of the world, it has its warts. But when you reach that point where a decision is to be made on where you will spend your retirement years, you will have to look long and hard to find any place that has so many advantages as a retirement site.

We hope this book will be a valuable guide in helping you to make that decision.

Retiring to British Columbia:

Kelowna across Okanagan Lake

A Quick Look

E ver since long distance travel became a practical reality for everyday Canadians, by train, car or plane, British Columbia has been a haven for those who sought to escape rigorous winters.

Since the end of World War II, B.C. has become more than a winter retreat and an increasingly popular retirement centre for other Canadians and even many non-Canadians - a haven from the rigors of their working lives.

Today, at least 12 per cent of British Columbia's 2.5 million residents are retired people over the age of 65. Because of that, governments and non-profit organizations and societies have become more attentive to the needs of the older segment of the population. Besides the services for seniors provided in all provinces by the federal government, British Columbia now offers a wide variety of additional services specifically aimed at serving its senior citizens.

The communities and areas highlighted in this book vary widely in the style of living they offer, the cost of housing and basic necessities, the services they have such as recreation and transportation, and in the type of weather you can expect. They are in this book because each one has something to offer. Our task has been to detail those strengths and point out any weaknesses. In the succeeding chapters, you should be able to find the British Columbia community that will best suit your needs and interests in your retirement years. In this chapter, however, we take a general look at what British Columbia has to offer in the way of climate, housing, medical services, transportation, recreation and entertainment. The chapters dealing with specific communities are organized similarly.

Climate

Climate is, without question, one of the major determining factors in our lifestyle. It dictates what we will wear, how we must equip ourselves for transportation, often how we must carry out our work and even our moods. Quite rightly, it ranks high on most people's checklist for choosing a place to live. And it is prominent among the reasons why other Canadians move to British Columbia.

Not all of British Columbia can boast about the climate. Parts of north-central and northern B.C. swelter in summer heat and shiver in a winter deep-freeze. Southern British Columbia, however, boasts a moderate, if often wet, climate. Here, there is weather to suit any taste, from the Pacific Coast's mild, wet and windy weather to the drier, sunny interior valleys where temperature extremes are within reason.

The climate in southwestern British Columbia is affected by the Pacific Ocean and the geographic diversity of its coastal areas, its mountain ranges and central plateaus. This diversity results in hours of sunshine, average rainfall and snow, and average temperatures that vary widely from city to city, even over a short distance.

Since the temperate climate is what attracts most people from the eastern part of the continent, the conditions of a given area should be a part of any decision to retire in British Columbia. Certain regions of the province are much more temperate than others. Even within those regions, there are significant variations in precipitation and hours of bright sunshine.

South Coastal Region

The climate here is subject to prevailing westerly winds off the Pacific. Weather is extremely changeable, both summer and winter. Lovers of the great outdoors should never be without rain gear, and warm protection in the winter, for those sudden rainstorms.

Summertime is usually reliable in serving up sunny, warm (not hot) weather with a frequent ocean breeze just to keep things civilized. Evenings can be cool, so a sweater, even in July, is not at all out of place.

In winter, the south coastal region is the most temperate in all of British Columbia. However, rainfall is frequent and predictable, and varies greatly in amounts depending on your location relative to local mountain ranges. Parts of this coast receive as much rainfall as the jungles of South America.

Vancouver receives much more rain than the eastern coast of Vancouver Island, including Victoria. Even within Vancouver, yearly rainfall in North Vancouver is greater than downtown because air rising over the city's scenic mountain backdrop loses its moisture as it cools.

The Okanagan

Away from the coast, the climate becomes more like that of the prairies both in summer and winter.

Climate in the Okanagan is greatly influenced by the high coastal mountain range which separates it from the coast. These mountains keep cool, moist coastal air from reaching the valley in summer and they funnel dry, cold air from the arctic down the corridors between the mountain ranges during the winter months.

Consequently, summers in the Okanagan Valley are typically hot with little wind. Precipitation any time of year, either as rain or snow, is low. For example, an average year on the coast will bring about 150 cm of rain while dropping only 31 cm on the Okanagan. Temperatures on the coast will typically range between -5 Celsius and +25 Celsius over the year, while temperatures in the south central interior vary between extremes of -18 Celsius in the winter to +32 Celsius in the summer.

Winters in the Okanagan region are not as cold or

windy as prairie winters. In fact, they can be very picturesque, with snow hanging heavily on evergreen boughs. So don't sell your snow shovel at your pre-moving garage sale. You'll need it in the Okanagan and, yes, even on the coast from time to time. There has been snow in Victoria, for example, every winter for the past six years, sometimes for only a few days but up to three or four weeks.

The North

As one moves northward, the climate changes yet again. For example, the Peace River district in the northeast corner of the province has an average winter temperature of -18 C and an average summer temperature of 15 Celsius. Extremes in this area range from a reported low of -29 Celsius to a high of 27 Celsius. The northern regions of the province have the lowest rates of precipitation but, for many, the extremes of winter and summer make it a less desirable place for retirement.

As you read the succeeding chapters, if a British Columbia community looks appealing to you, check in Appendix E at the back of the book for important climatic indicators and compare them with the climate you know right now. That will help you visualize what you might be moving to.

Housing

For those who want to buy a home in British Columbia, property values vary greatly from region to region and, to a lesser extent, within a particular region.

Whether or not you will have money left over in the course of selling elsewhere in Canada and buying in British Columbia will depend on your individual situation and that's why we've included some comparative tables at the back, so you can compare for yourself. The succeeding chapters contain some general comments on the nature of each of the housing markets.

Once you have bought a home in B.C., there is an annual provincial homeowner grant of $380, paid directly by the provincial government to the municipality where you live, to offset your taxes. For homeowners over 65, the grant was $630 in 1986.

For seniors living on a very limited income, there is a provincial government program called Shelter Aid For Elderly Renters (SAFER). It provides a direct cash payment to assist in the payment of rent for those 65 or older who are receiving the federal Old Age pension and are paying over 30 per cent of their monthly income on rent. To qualify, you must have resided in B.C. two years prior to application, or have lived in the province for a continuous five-year period at any time.

In addition, the B.C. Housing Management Commission and some non-profit organizations operate low rental housing for seniors. Further information can be obtained through:

Shelter Aid For Elderly Renters
Parliament Buildings
Victoria, B.C. V8V 1W4
Telephone: 687-4331
Office hours: 8:30 a.m. to 4:30 p.m.,
Monday through Friday

If you do not wish to purchase a home or rent, there is a homesharing program available through SAFER that finds compatible people to share accommodation. Cooperative housing is another alternative. Its main advantages and disadvantages are profiled on page 72.

The Ministry of Human Resources also has a program of volunteer senior citizen counsellors who can aid in such matters as housing, consumer affairs, nutrition, discounts, activities and the law.

B.C. Ferry

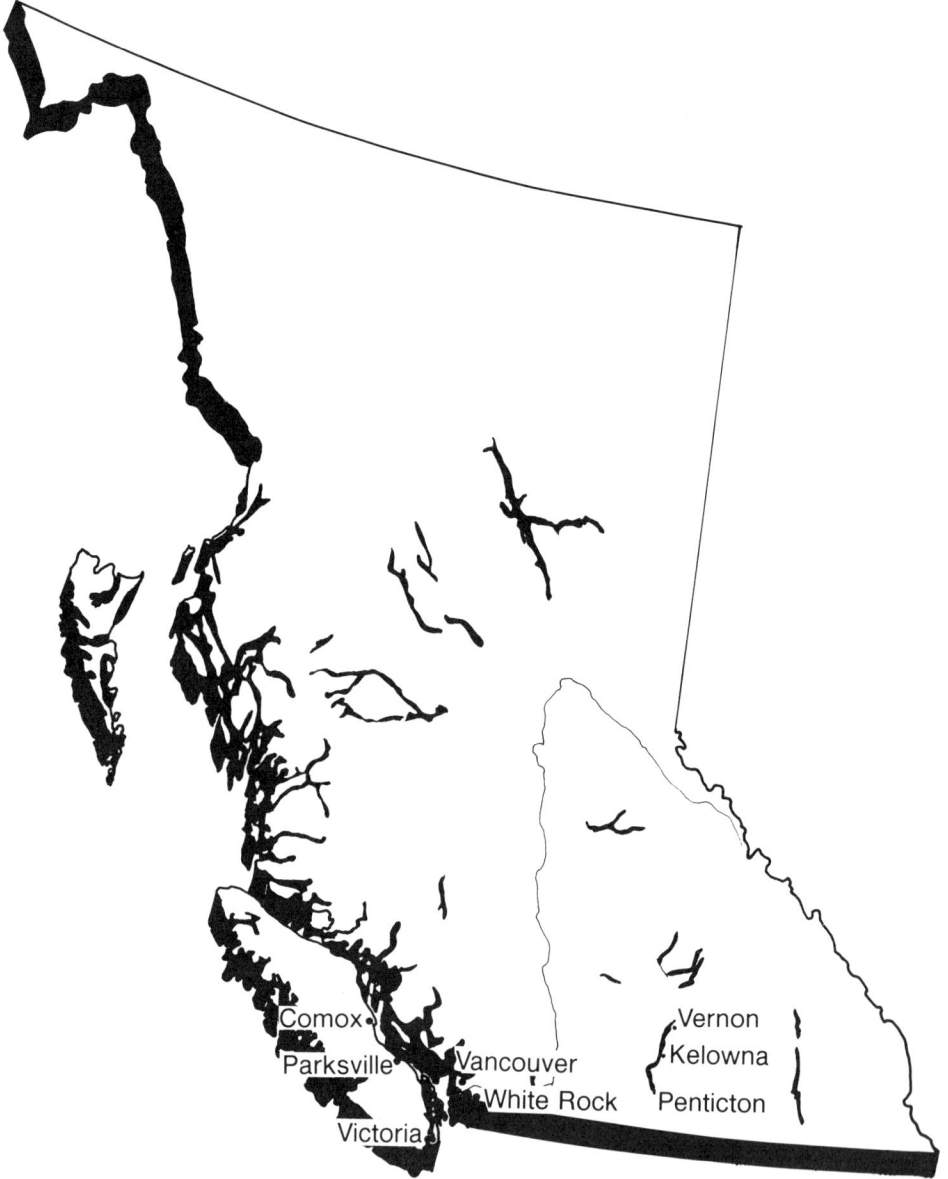

Comox
Parksville
Vancouver
White Rock
Victoria
Vernon
Kelowna
Penticton

Medical Services

British Columbia has an extensive network of acute care hospitals, long-term care facilities and specialized medical services.

Still, like anywhere else, the health care system has its problems. Those awaiting elective surgery can and do wait months for it. Getting into a long-term care facility may take months unless you are willing to pay the surcharge of entering a private facility.

Those retiring from provinces where there are no medicare insurance premiums, user fees for hospital stays, or health care surcharges on income tax will have to take such expenses into account when budgetting.

You must also ask yourself vital questions about your health care needs to ensure a smooth adjustment in your move. Ask your family doctor what he or she knows about B.C. health care. Ask yourself what kinds of health care you use now. What is the current state of your personal health? What services might you need in the future? Will they be available in the B.C. retirement community you are considering? As in other provinces, not all services are available everywhere. This section and the community chapters later on will help you sort out what is available.

Medical Insurance

It is vital for new arrivals to the province to make immediate application for coverage by the Medical Services Plan. It provides basic medical coverage and is available to new residents on the first day of the third month after arrival, providing application has been made upon arrival. The plan in your own province will provide you medical coverage during this waiting period.

Subscribers are required to pay premiums of about $400 per year per couple. A premium reduction of up to 90 per cent is available to those whose taxable income in the previous year was below a given level. Ask for a Premium Assistance application from the Medical Plan since most seniors receiving only the Old Age Pension/Guaranteed Income Supplement are eligible for this subsidy.

Covered by the plan are:

☐ the services of a physician at home, in hospital or institutions;
☐ specialists, psychiatrists, anaesthetists
☐ X-ray and laboratory services
☐ dental and oral surgery.

Limited additional services include chiropractic, naturopathic, physiotherapy, podiatry, optometry, orthoptic and orthodontic. Even massage practitioners are covered by the plan.

If you are out of the province and require medical treatment, reimbursement is limited to the schedule of fees paid here in B.C. Most people buy additional private medical insurance when travelling outside of Canada.

The B.C. Hospital Plan covers care in B.C.'s acute care wards and specialized care hospitals. It covers diagnostic, surgical and treatment procedures ordered by a physician or medical specialist. Patients must pay a user fee at hospitals: $8 per day for basic accommodation at this writing; $15.50 per day in a long-term care facility. Fees are slightly higher for emergency ward service, acute care wards, private rooms and day surgery/outpatient services.

Because it is such a wide-ranging and complex health plan, you'd be wise to obtain all the literature available and application forms free of charge from:

Medical Services Plan of B.C.
1515 Blanshard Street
Victoria, B.C. V8W 3C8
Telephone 386-3166
Office hours: 8:30 a.m. to 4:30 p.m.,
Monday through Friday.

Pharmacare

If you have lived in British Columbia for three months, you are eligible for Pharmacare. Applicants must also be enrolled in the Medical Services Plan. Applications for Pharmacare may be found at any pharmacy.

Pharmacare coverage is free of premiums and covers prescribed drugs, insulin syringes for diabetics, some prosthetic appliances and ostomy supplies. It does not pay for over-the-counter drugs, even if a physician prescribes them.

For those under 65 years, the plan will reimburse 80 per cent of eligible expenses above $200 in each year. You must pay for the drugs and can start claiming reimbursement from Pharmacare when you have exceeded $200. That may be part way through the year for those with conditions requiring on-going, expensive drug treatment.

For those over 65, all eligible drugs are free and you don't have to pay first and collect later. Through a numbered Pharmacare card which proves your eligibility, the provincial government provides full payment directly to the pharmacist. The Pharmacare card is also the key to a range of other perks for seniors, such as reduced fares and admissions, because it is the standard proof of age for seniors.

Further information on Pharmacare is available, free of charge, from:

Pharmacare
Parliament Buildings
Victoria, B.C. V8V 1W4
Telephone: 387-3724
Office hours: 8:30 a.m. to 4:30 p.m.,
                    Monday through Friday.

Ambulance

Ambulance services are provided on land, sea and air. Where a local ambulance service does not exist, you may contact the nearest RCMP detachment in an emergency. Individuals are charged the same for all three modes of transportation - $28 for the first 40 kilometres and 29 cents for every extra kilometre to a maximum of $180.

The Cost of Living

When you travel to another area, comparing the cost of goods and services with those in your current hometown is always a matter of interest. When you move, it's not just interesting, it's important.

Getting reliable statistics is difficult because prices change over time and what you get for the money is not always easily compared. Given those caveats,

On crossing the 49th

For Americans considering retirement in British Columbia, the perceived difficulties of moving to another country may outweigh the attractions. But such a move is really not that difficult.

As with any government function, immigration involves a certain amount of red tape. It can be frustrating if you're unsure of how to proceed.

The least-complicated way to move into Canada on a permanent basis is to apply for landed immigrant status or permanent residency. It cost $125 to apply.

As a retired American citizen coming into Canada without any relatives in Canada, you must be able to prove that you are of 'good health and character', a maximum of 55 years old, and able to provide 'sufficient funds' to support yourself. The criteria for judging good health, good character and sufficient funds are open to some interpretation by immigration officials, so we can't list definitive criteria here for you.

If you have a Canadian relative to sponsor your immigration to Canada, he or she must agree to guarantee your support for 10 years. In this case, you don't have to prove you have sufficient funds to support yourself and you can be up to 60 years old when you apply.

Once you have immigrated to Canada and have obtained landed immigrant or permanent

however, we can try to give you an idea of how your expenses might add up.

The major part of any personal budget is accommodation.

If you plan to buy, the average selling price for all types of residential accommodation in British Columbia in 1985 was $89,152. But that figure is a very crude indicator of housing prices.

Let's look at the standard bungalow type of house and compare a few areas of B.C. In July 1986, Royal

resident status, life becomes comparatively simple. As a permanent resident of B.C., you are eligible for the government-operated Medical Services Plan at a cost of approximately $400 per year per couple. Once you apply, there is a three-month waiting period before the plan takes effect. Private agencies offer limited coverage for health emergencies and hospitalization during this waiting period.

If you are not a permanent resident, you are not eligible for the government-operated plan. Your only alternative then is an American medical plan or private Canadian insurance.

If you spend a major portion of each year in Canada and have some evidence of the permanency of your stay here, such as owning or renting a home, you qualify as a permanent resident for Canadian income tax purposes. That covers both American income and income from Canadian sources.

If you want to purchase property in Canada and require a mortgage, Canadian banks require a statement of your income and employment status from your employer. If you are in business for yourself, they require income tax returns for your business for the preceding three years. If you are already retired, they require a statement from your banker. They also require these things of Canadian citizens.

LePage, a real estate firm which regularly conducts a cross-Canada survey, estimated the fair market value of a bungalow in Kelowna at $70,000, in Burnaby at $116,000, in the Kerrisdale area of Vancouver at $210,000 and in Victoria at $90,000.

To buy a standard condominium in Kelowna in July 1986 would be about $40,000, according to Royal LePage, $58,000 in Burnaby, $145,000 in Kerrisdale and $61,000 in Victoria.

Renting houses in those areas would vary between $500 (Kelowna) and $1,500 (Kerrisdale). Two-bedroom apartment rentals in Kelowna in July 1986 averaged $394, $571 in Vancouver and $480 in Victoria.

See the tables in the appendices at the back for a broader view of the housing market.

Property taxes on the average detached bungalow in Kelowna in 1986 were about $900 in 1986, about $1,100 in Penticton, $1,160 in Vernon and $1,100 in Victoria. They varied between $1,100 and $1,700 in the various areas of Greater Vancouver.

The next major expense is food. According to a 'nutritious food basket' put together and priced out by Statistics Canada, it would have cost a family of four in Victoria $105 per week in June 1986 for a nutritionally-sound diet. For a couple in their 60s, a nutritious diet would have cost $50.46 per week in Victoria. The corresponding costs for Vancouver are slightly lower at $102.22 and $49.11. Food prices in other Vancouver Island communities would tend to be slightly higher than Victoria while food prices in the Okanagan are on a par with the Lower Mainland.

You may want to check your own food bill against the food basket price in your province in the appendix at the back. That way, you'll know how the figures above relate to you.

You must heat your home and run your household appliances, like the clothes dryer and the fridge. Hydro for operating appliances, excluding the water heater, does not vary widely between locations in B.C. and averages about $30 per month for a couple living in a detached dwelling, according to B.C. Hydro figures.

Heating your water will vary with the amount you use, of course, but also with your method of heating it. Natural gas is the least expensive and costs about $100 per year. But because there is no natural gas pipeline to Vancouver Island, it is not a cheap or viable option for island residents. If a distribution system exists in your area, the natural gas that must be brought to the island by boat to heat your water will cost you about $250 per year.

Heating your water electrically would be about $190 per year, according to 1986 Hydro estimates. Oil can be the most expensive if world oil prices are high. In 1984, your oil bill for water heating would have been over $200. In 1986, it would have been about $165.

The cost of heating your home will vary on two counts: how cold the winters are in your area and which fuel you burn. Remember, natural gas is costly on Vancouver Island and cheap on the mainland. And remember also that the price of oil is not as stable as the price of electricity.

Here is Hydro's comparison of the costs for three fuels in three areas of the province, based on prices in mid-1986. The estimates are based on heating a 1,200 square foot, moderately-well insulated single-storey home with double-glazed windows. (Be sure to check the windows in your new home. Many older homes on the coast have single-pane glass.)

Estimated Yearly Heating Costs

	Electricity	Oil	Natural Gas
Vancouver Island	$470	$485	$730
Lower Mainland	$495	$510	$355
Southern Interior	$660	$695	$395

Another charge that returns every month is for telephone. B.C. Telephone Company bases its rates on a charge for the line and a separate charge for the type of telephone you select. Both vary. Line charges depend on the size of the free-calling area in your community - that is, the size of area in which you can call without long-distance charges. In the Lower Mainland, that area will be substantially larger than, say, for a community like Parksville. A line rate in White Rock in the Lower Mainland, for example, is about $16 per month for a private residence. In other areas of the province, it can be as little as $5.65. Telephone rentals vary between $2 and $6 per month, depending on the type you pick.

Transportation

Holders of Pharmacare cards for seniors pay a reduced fare on transit systems in 23 B.C. communi-

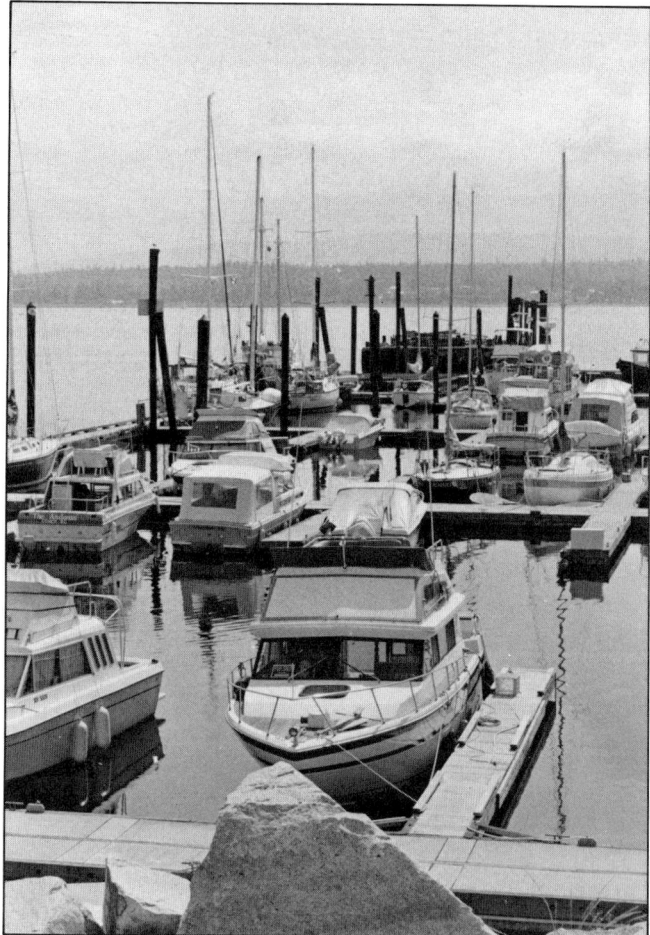

Marina at Comox

ties, including Victoria and Vancouver.

Pharmacare cards also get you free passage on B.C. ferries Monday through Thursday (except for statutory holidays) and provide a 25 per cent reduction on B.C. Rail fares. Air Canada and Via Rail also offer discounts on fares and there is a $5 reduction on the cost of a driver's licence. Driver examinations are free for cardholders.

There are also transportation breaks for recipients of the Guaranteed Annual Income for the Needy, known as GAIN. This provincial program ensures a guaranteed minimum income level for B.C. residents receiving federal Old Age Security, Guaranteed Income Supplement and federal Spouse's Allowance. GAIN also provides travel without charge on all transit systems.

A special transit service is available for those who cannot use the regular system. This service uses vans specially equipped to handle wheelchairs and other handicapped individuals, and provides service from your door right to your destination for a nominal charge. To qualify for this service, you must be receiving GAIN for Handicapped or have a medically qualified disability, not necessarily a permanent one.

Recreation and Entertainment

The Pharmacare card entitles the holder to free or reduced admission to provincial parks, some art galleries, live theatre and movie houses, as well as reduced rates at many hotels and restaurants.

British Columbia communities are well stocked with social organizations and clubs to serve the recreational needs of seniors. Many are funded through the federal New Horizons program. Others are associated with churches or are simply groups of seniors who have come together for a common purpose.

In many cities, there are community recreation

centres with programs designed specifically for seniors' participation. There is no shortage of opportunity to make new friends and enjoy social companionship in British Columbia.

The best source of information is a local telephone book, Chamber of Commerce, churches and recreation centres.

For those who want to further their education or become involved in some vocational activity, most colleges and universities have programs for the mature student who does not meet the usual university or college requirements. In addition, senior citizens can usually attend university courses free of charge, regardless of whether they are studying for a degree or taking personal interest courses. Contact the registrars of the individual institutions for more detailed information.

Suggested Retirement Communities

This book confines itself to dealing with those cities, towns and communities where retired persons appear to find themselves most at ease but, at the same time, close to the amenities they require. In other words, the most popular retirement centres in the province.

They are the most popular for good reason and we will describe those reasons briefly here and then in detail in succeeding sections.

Vancouver - Centre of British Columbia's commercial and business activities, Vancouver is the province's largest metropolitan area, offering all the amenities of other large North America cities plus unmatched scenery all around it.

Vancouver weather is mild and damp in winter, with occasional snow which quickly melts, and warm and breezy in summer, without becoming oppressively hot.

The city is ringed by a number of suburban municipalities, including Burnaby, Richmond, Surrey and North Vancouver.

Housing costs in Greater Vancouver, a term which includes the suburbs, are generally higher than elsewhere in the province.

Excellent highways and public transportation offer easy access to mountain and wilderness country close by, with excellent fishing, hunting and camping. Ferry access to Vancouver Island is frequent and reliable and road access to the Okanagan Valley has been improved with the new Coquihalla Highway.

White Rock - About 40 kilometres south of Vancouver, White Rock is right on the American border. It is generally a less-expensive place to live than Vancouver. It is also a favorite summer resort area for Lower Mainland residents, so it is crowded in summer and quiet in winter. If you don't mind the summer crowds attracted to its warm water beaches, it is a delightful place to live. Residential areas in White Rock are generally situated on large areas of wooded land, much of it only now being developed.

Pier at White Rock

Victoria - British Columbia's political capital and seat of government, Victoria is located at the southern tip of Vancouver Island. It is less than 160 kilometres from Seattle, Wash. and is well-serviced to both Seattle and Vancouver by both sea and air transport.

Housing is less expensive than in Vancouver and it is a much quieter city than Vancouver. It has several very pleasant residential areas both in Victoria proper and in its surrounding municipalities.

Victoria has a year-round mild climate, and while wet in winter, it receives less rain than Vancouver.

The Gulf Islands - These islands, seemingly adrift in the Strait of Georgia, provide some of the most breathtaking marine scenery anywhere to the thousands of B.C. Ferry passengers that sail among them annually between Vancouver Island and the mainland.

The 16 islands - Saltspring, Galiano, Mayne, Saturna and North and South Pender are the main ones - conjure up romantic images of idyllic island life, an almost spendid isolation. And there's no doubt they attract an eclectic, if sometimes curious, mix of immigrant residents.

But beware. Gulf Island life is not for everyone.

Qualicum-Parksville - About 160 kilometres north of Victoria, these two delightful little resort communities nestle together on the east coast of Vancouver Island. Housing and household costs are less than in Vancouver or Victoria and the weather is milder and sunnier.

Those features, its warm coastal waters and wonderful salmon fishing make it a very busy summer vacation spot. The nearest transportation centre to Vancouver is Nanaimo, about 40 kilometres to the south, or Victoria.

For the more rural type of living, it is a choice location.

Courtenay-Comox - The Comox
Valley is north of Parksville-Qualicum on the sheltered east coast of Vancouver Island. Warm waters, sandy beaches, mild temperatures and little wind make this an attractive area for retired people of all ages.

This is scenic country, with the coastal mountains rising above the waters of Georgia Strait. There is little industry, save for small farms and tourism. Real estate is reasonable and the lifestyle is informal.

Okanagan Valley - Five or six hours
drive inland from Vancouver, the Okanagan Valley has three major centres: Penticton, at the south end of Okanagan Lake; Kelowna, about halfway up the lake, and Vernon, at its northern tip.

Weather in the valley is excellent. Summers are warm and breezy. Winters, colder than the coastal areas, are usually sunny and crisp. Snowfall is reasonable.

Warm lake waters attract thousands of summer vacationers.

Housing and living costs are lower than on the Lower Mainland or Victoria and the Okanagan is well-served by air transport and an excellent highway system offering access north, east and west.

These are the communities that would have most appeal to people deciding to retire in British Columbia.

They are all located in a moderate temperature belt. They are all physically attractive and all offer most of the amenities and comforts that should be expected. But they are not all the same. The succeeding chapters will give you a more detailed look the differences in lifestyle in each of them.

If you have a disability. . .

Disabilities of any type or severity present special problems that can easily become frustrating if you lack the knowledge or resources to deal with them.

Most urban centres in British Columbia are aware of the problems faced by disabled citizens, especially where there is a significant population of seniors.

In Victoria and Vancouver, most public buildings are ramped for wheelchair access, some auditory traffic signals for blind pedestrians are provided and some facilities, such as universities and some government buildings, have Braille identifiers on the doors and elevators.

In addition to physical facilities, there are a number of societies and associations that provide special services for those with disabilities. For example, there are a variety of speech and hearing clinics throughout the province (except Vancouver) which require a doctor's certificate for initial placement. There is no charge for the diagnostic test but hearing aids can cost between $300 and $350.

The Western Institute for the Deaf is a nonprofit organization located in Vancouver and Victoria. In addition to testing and assessing hearing, it provides counselling and training for hearing-impaired persons in lip-reading and sign language. Charges for these services are nominal.

For both elderly and handicapped persons, transportation presents special problems. 'Handydart' services provide transportation in Vancouver, Victoria and eight other urban centres in the province. Handydart provides a door-to-door, wheelchair-accessible bus service for those who cannot use regular public transit. To be eligible for the service, a doctor's certificate is required.

Mobility aids such as canes, crutches, walkers, wheelchairs or commodes, can be obtained temporarily or permanently from the Canadian Red Cross, the Kinsmen Rehabilitation Foundation, or the Vancouver Masonic Services Bureau. If you are unsure of how to use any aids that you may require, your local community health unit can provide training. In addition, the South Vancouver Senior's Network provides information on mobility aids and maintains a registry of persons wishing to buy, sell, give or loan an aid.

The Canadian Institute for the Blind has branches in Vancouver, Victoria, Kelowna, New Westminster and Prince George. They offer training and counselling for the visually impaired that emphasizes adjustment and making use of other senses such as hearing and touch. These services are extended to the spouse of the visually-impaired individual.

The CNIB operates a talking, recorded library, with a loan service. If you live in a community that does not have a CNIB office, all public libraries have a reasonable collection of recorded books, or they can locate them for you. If you live in a very remote area, the Audiobook Service at 150 - 4946 Canada Way, V5G 4H7 in Burnaby can help you.

In addition to these 'traditional' disabilities, there are a number of voluntary, non-profit organizations that provide various kinds of support, focusing on different aspects of health - diabetes, hemophilia, arthritis, strokes, Alzheimer's disease, and mental health. If you are community-minded, and disabled, you may consider becoming involved with the B.C. Coalition for the Disabled, which promotes the interests and needs of the disabled through government lobbying. Specific issues include housing, transportation, training and benefits.

When you put it all together, it seems to come up White Rock.

Not only does White Rock have a high proportion of retired residents, but it has services that reflect the power of that group combined with easy-living weather and location.

It has access to Vancouver for night life and to the U.S. for savings. The islands are close, as is the airport. It is the perfect launching pad if you still want to travel, and a great stay-at-home location if travel is behind you.

No community can ever be for everyone but on average, White Rock comes out ahead.

- Mark Krasnick

Victoria gets my vote as the best place in Canada for retired people of any age, and let's include working people and children, too.

The short story on Victoria is it's a small (yet big enough) urban community, with a cosmopolitan (not just British) atmosphere in a gorgeous physical setting with a very civilized climate.

I hate shovelling snow (so don't give me the Okanagan), am not keen on either big cities or small towns (that knocks out Vancouver and the small island towns) but occasionally partake of the social amenities which a city can offer (Victoria's right there).

- Don Lindenberg

Between the lines

In researching this book, some recurring observations emerged from the hundreds of interviews with retired British Columbians. And while it's hard to group them with the hard facts and descriptive material in other parts of the book, it would still be useful to detail some of them.

For example, weather predominates as the major factor influencing people's decision to move to B.C. for their retirement years. People move to British Columbia because of the weather, they move around the province because of the weather and they stay in British Columbia because of the weather.

The major factor that determines how happy retired people are once they get here is the availability of friends - either old or new. We found that people who left good friends behind and were unable to make new ones are the unhappiest. The observation seems almost self-evident but, still, it's a point worth pondering. Consider how important friends are to your happiness and consider a new neighborhood in terms of "people".

Housing options also figure prominently in the happiness of retired persons. Many people we interviewed regretted having tied their money up in a house. It left them with fewer choices, made travel financially more difficult and consumed large amounts of what they thought would be spare time. Many were unhappy with the neighborhood they chose.

To avoid those problems, many seniors advised that newcomers rent before buying or consider less expensive options like mobile home parks, condominiums or retirement communities.

Retirement communities around the province offer condominium, mobile home or apartment living, usually on a purchase basis. These communities offer recreational facilities, both social and physical, and living accommodation that is designed for seniors, such as wide hallways, one-level living, raised wall outlets for electricity. Older retirees expressed a greater degree of happiness in such complexes.

Recreation also ranked high on the list of factors which determine how happy people are with the choices they made in their retirement move. Think about what you want to be doing when you're retired. Do you want to be near golf courses? Shopping? Fishing? People? Travel?

Some random observations. We found that:

☐ people are happiest in centres that are the same size, or smaller, than the one they left.

☐ people over 60 participate more in organized social activity,

☐ people in lower income groups were less happy in large centres than those in smaller centres.

☐ people over 65 were happier in retirement communities than retired persons under 65.

☐ people who move initially to a centre larger than the one they left end up moving to a smaller one.

☐ independent seniors use recreation centres the most.

☐ people over 65 living in retirement communities were more content with their lifestyle than retirees of the same age living independently.

☐ widow/ers in a lower income bracket living in large centres were the unhappiest of all retirees.

☐ widowers (not widows) use retirement drop-in centres the most.

☐ rural Albertans and some Manitobans tend to retire to the interior, Americans gravitate to Vancouver, British retire to Vancouver Island, and people from Saskatchewan tend to move to the island.

For those who want to live in a smaller centre, Penticton seems to offer the best of all worlds - a small town atmosphere with many features of larger interesting centres. It's busy in the summer, but not crowded, the weather is pleasant in all seasons, there are always things to do. It would appeal to retirees because of its services and bus system.

Of course, it has it's disadvantages. For a small town, it's too sprawling and the various seniors' centres are spread out. A car is definitely an asset. And if you want to avoid snow at all costs, Penticton is not for you.

However, for a small town, it has a lot to offer its citizens. It's one of the prettiest towns in the interior.

- Carmen Farrell

Downtown Vancouver from
Spanish Banks

Vancouver

For urban-oriented people who want to be where the action is, Vancouver is the place to settle in B.C.

Planted on a rolling peninsula between Burrard Inlet and False Creek, Vancouver's urban core has grown into the cultural, financial, commercial and industrial centre of the province. Its suburban communities have gradually filled in much of the surrounding hills and Fraser River delta with residential and commercial development.

Those things are not unique among large North American cities. But Vancouver's combination of scenic coastal mountains, placid inland ocean waters and moderate climate are unique, attracting people of all ages from all over the globe to this metropolis.

Vancouver is one of the major seaports on North America's Pacific coast. It is the railhead for Canada's two major railways and the site of one of the largest and busiest international airports in the country.

More than 400,000 people live in Vancouver itself. But when you include the suburban communities in what is known as Greater Vancouver, the population is about 1.2 million.

Those surrounding cities and municipalities were, as recently as 25 years ago, clearly-defined individual communities. But rapid development, beginning shortly after World War II, has made the whole area from Burrard Inlet on the north to the Fraser River on the south into one massive, interlocked urban community.

Vancouver's main business and shopping district hugs Burrard Inlet on the northern edge of this urban area. It is a relatively small area, about 20 blocks by 25 blocks, and is densely developed with highrise office, commercial and apartment or condominium buildings.

Weather

Vancouver's climate might be described as west coast moderate. That means it rarely experiences extremes and it rains a lot.

The average annual rainfall varies considerably over the Lower Mainland area, increasing as you get closer to the North Shore mountains. For example, at the airport in Richmond south of the city, average annual precipitation is about 111 cm. In downtown Vancouver, that average rises to 154 cm and just across Burrard Inlet in North Vancouver, annual precipitation is 186 cm, rising to almost 200 cm per year at the higher levels of the North Shore mountains. You can compare those figures with your own area on the table in the weather appendix.

The heaviest rains fall in the first five and last three months of the year. Annual snowfall is about 10 cm at the airport, very wet and very heavy. The average annual temperature is 10 degrees Celsius.

Despite the rainy statistics, Vancouver on a clear day, winter or summer, easily qualifies as one of the most beautiful cities on the continent. Part of that beauty, the North Shore mountain range, is also responsible for prolonging rainy spells by blocking cloud movement to the interior. Still, Vancouver is sheltered from the open ocean and escapes much of the heavy seasonal wind that hits other coastal communities. And weather statistics show the city gets a respectable 1,700 hours of sunshine each year.

"I moved to British Columbia because of my health. I just got tired of the snow and cold. It just became too much for me, so I just said 'Ida, you're retiring. Just move somewhere different."

- Ida, from Montreal living in Vancouver

Housing

As with most large, busy cities, Vancouver tends to be more expensive than smaller communities around the province. Inattentive shoppers will find themselves paying premium prices in the city for everything from housing to hardwares.

But that need not be the case. Even in the downtown core of Vancouver, a careful survey of the market and an eye for bargains can make it an acceptable and exciting place to live at a moderate price.

The core is just a very small part of the city. Vancouver is divided into several loosely-defined neighborhoods, where the character of the housing and its cost can vary greatly. The neighborhoods have a good sense of community and are, in some ways, a series of self-sufficient entities despite the lack of visible boundaries.

Outside of the city, the suburban municipalities such as North and West Vancouver, Richmond, Delta, Surrey, Burnaby and New Westminster offer their own brand of lifestyle and housing.

The choice depends largely on the character of the neighborhood you seek, the money that is available for housing, the amenities you seek in the immediate area and on how much importance you attach to living close to the city's core area.

Of course, there is no substitute for visiting an area in making the decision about where one would like to live. But further on in this section, we describe briefly many of the neighborhoods of Vancouver, to give you a starting point for further research and perhaps some basis for eliminating neighborhoods that are totally inappropriate to your needs, desires and financial capacities. In an appendix at the back, you can compare actual selling prices of homes in Vancouver at a specific date to prices at that time in the area where you now live.

Another pipeline for information on housing in the Lower Mainland is a tabloid newspaper called the Real Estate Weekly. It is distributed through the real estate agencies that advertise in it and is a great place to get an idea of what kind of money is required for a particular type of house.

Unfortunately, you cannot subscribe to Real Estate Weekly. The only way of getting it is by picking it up at one of those advertising real estate agents. But you may be able to make connection through an interprovincial network at your own real estate agent, or if you have relatives or acquaintances in the Lower Mainland, they might be willing to send it to you. It will only cost the price of postage, since the paper is free.

The paper is actually seven different papers, published for the various areas of the Lower Mainland - Vancouver West Side, Vancouver East-Burnaby, Richmond, North Shore, Coquitlam-Maple Ridge-New Westminster, Surrey-North Delta, and Langley-

We see where you're coming from

If you are an immigrant to Canada, you will not be alone in British Columbia.

Fully one quarter of British Columbians are immigrants. Most of them were born in the United States or Britain. But there are sizable contingents of German, Scandinavian, French, Dutch and Asian people, too.

In urban centres like Vancouver, some ethnics groups settle in 'pockets' of the city. Vancouver has its Chinatown, Little Italy (a clustered Italian community) and a significant East Indian culture. Victoria has its own Chinatown and one of the largest Asian populations outside of the far east.

Ancestors of today's British Columbians come from all over the globe. Almost 60 per cent of the province's population claims British heritage, but there are significant groups of other national backgrounds.

Native Indians form a significant segment of the West Coast population, both on Vancouver Island and the Lower Mainland. Much of West Coast art and even architecture borrows bits and pieces from the art of the Haida, Kwakiutl and Nootka tribes of the coastal regions.

Sixty per cent of British Columbia's 2.9 million people them live in the urban areas of Vancouver and Victoria. If you include the suburban areas surrounding these two cities, the proportion increases to 75 per cent.

Cloverdale-Abbotsford.

There are a substantial number of retirement homes and housing projects for seniors in Greater Vancouver. Some of them have a direct religious affiliation. Some are sponsored by a church but make no demands on tenants concerning religious activity. Rents in most cases are reasonable and depend to some degree on services offered other than accom-

Robson Square

modation. Some have nursing services, others do not. For specific information, contact: the B.C. Old Age Pensioners' Organization, Box 37, Whaletown, Cortes Island, V0P 1Z0, Telephone 935-6315, the Council of Senior Citizen Organizations, 5115 Frances Street, Burnaby, B.C., V5B 1T2, or the Senior Citizens' Association of B.C., 2336 Dollarton Highway, North Vancouver, B.C. V7H 1A8, Telephone 929-1567.

Housing cooperatives offer an alternative to buying or renting. In the Greater Vancouver area, there are about 100 housing cooperatives offering a variety of housing from apartments and group townhouses to single family homes. Waiting lists to get in are common. See page 72 for a profile of cooperative housing in B.C. and for further specific information, contact the Cooperative Housing Federation of B.C., 4676 Main Street, Vancouver, B.C. V5V 3R7, Telephone 879-5111.

"We moved to B.C. because we had some friends and family in the interior. But we didn't realize how little we'd see them, so we rely mainly on friends we've made in the city.
"But it's hard. John's disability, he's in a wheelchair, just makes it that much more difficult to get around so we don't get out as much as we thought we would. We like our neighborhood but find it expensive and lonely.
"Kerrisdale is lonely because the people are so hard to get to know, even now, after 13 years."

- Retired couple from Winnipeg

Medical Services

Vancouver has major acute care hospitals offering some of the most up-to-date medical treatment in the world. The University of B.C. hospital is one of the country's leading research facilities.

However, patients can experience lengthy waits for elective surgery at Vancouver hospitals due to a combination of factors; a shortage of available beds for surgery (especially during summer holidays or Christmas), a shortage of surgeons or specialized nursing staff during holiday periods and the fact that some surgeons have very lengthy waiting lists of their own.

The City of Vancouver offers a host of public health services which parallel those offered elsewhere in the province by the Ministry of Health. These include homemaker and home nursing services, public health nursing and a variety of fitness and lifestyle programs for seniors.

Shopping and Transportation

Daily living costs in Vancouver are on a par with other urban locations in British Columbia. The various residential communities are well-stocked with shopping and personal services. There is everything from small corner convenience stores to huge shopping malls with acres of parking.

Transportation, because of the size of the city, is more expensive than most other B.C. cities. Vancouver buses offer frequent service throughout the city and its suburban communities. At this writing, single zone fares for adults are $1.15 while seniors ride for 60 cents. The city and surrounding municipalities are divided up into transit zones. Increased fares are charged when you travel long distances through more than one zone. Day passes are also available for $3 ($1.50 for seniors) which permit unlimited travel on the whole system for an entire day from 9:30 a.m. until the last bus stops.

The day passes are also valid on the seabus which operates between Vancouver and North Vancouver and the new elevated, automated commuter train, called Skytrain, which operates between Vancouver and New Westminster.

Recreation, Entertainment, News

Because recreation and entertainment opportunities in the Greater Vancouver area are so numerous and diverse, we will limit this description to a number of activities that would interest retired persons (on the assumption that most of them can wait until they arrive before locating the nearest waterslides and rollercoasters).

"Well, there's the seniors drop-in centre on Thirty-Seventh, plus I attend the occasional lecture at UBC and I do a bit of volunteer work at the West End community centre. I couldn't function without a car, though. I think you need a car to be active in Vancouver."

Vancouver has an extensive network of community centres that have well-developed programs designed to appeal to retired people. Activities typically include bridge, bingo, carpet bowling, dances and fitness classes. Special events are organized around things like whale-watching and other boat trips. Besides the programs aimed at seniors, the centres usually have activities for all age groups and these are normally available to seniors at a discount of 30 per cent.

There are at least 25 such centres and quite likely one of them will be not far from where you might choose to live. Membership fees can be as low as $2 per year, though there are usually fees for individual activities.

There are three provincial community organizations for seniors the B.C. Old Age Pensioners Organization, the Council of Senior Citizen Organizations, or the Senior Citizens' Association of B.C. These organizations are worth joining as a source of information about seniors' activities. Their addresses are listed above under housing.

There are at least five lawn bowling clubs. Typical of them is Kerrisdale Lawn Bowling Club, where membership fees, once you are approved by an instructor to join, are $40 per year. Members care for the green on a volunteer basis.

There are dozens of golf courses around the Lower Mainland, too numerous to list them all here. The handful of choice courses include Capilano Golf and Country Club, Shaughnessy Golf and Country Club, Vancouver Golf Club, Marine Drive Golf Club, Point Grey Golf and Country Club, Quilchena Golf and Country Club and Richmond Country Club.

Unfortunately, it is not easy or cheap to get on these courses. They are private and one must normally be introduced by a member in order to play. If you can get on Capilano, for example, green fees are $75 per round. Becoming a member at Capilano will require some patience. When this was written, no new members had been accepted for seven months and none of the 40 applications on file were going to

"We bought a condominium in Richmond which we really enjoy. We find it ideal for our needs because we know it's secure when we're away from home. We've also found the people of Richmond to be very sociable and we've both already made some good friends."

- Retired Richmond couple

be processed for at least another six months. A social membership, the first step toward full playing membership, requires in initiation fee of $6,000 plus an extra $1,000 for a spouse and about $900 each year. That entitles you to a maximum of two rounds per month. Full playing membership nets an initiation fee of $15,000, $3,000 extra for a spouse and yearly fees of $1,560.

Capilano is at the top end of the scale in terms of playing costs, but several other private clubs are in the same range. And a pleasant round of golf can be had at any of the other numerous semi-private and public courses for much less money.

Entertainment is in abundant supply in Greater Vancouver. The city is large enough to attract internationally-known entertainers frequently and city nightclubs weekly feature first-class professional entertainers, both local and from farther afield. Two major professional sports teams are based in Vancouver - the B.C. Lions football team and the Vancouver Canucks hockey team. Both are well-patronized.

Vancouver has a diverse array of newspapers, many serving special interest or ethnic groups but most tied to a geographic area within the city or the Lower Mainland area.

The two major daily newspapers serving not only the Lower Mainland but other parts of the province as well are the Vancouver Sun and The Province. Though they operate from the same building and are both owned by the Southam newspaper chain, the papers have decidedly different characters. The Province is a tabloid and seemingly likes to play the sassy tabloid role. The Sun plays its news a little straighter on a broad-sheet format.

Both papers have extensive classified sections that can fill you in on housing availability and price. For a subscription to either paper, address your letter to the circulation department of your choice, 2250 Granville Street, Vancouver, B.C., V6H 3G2, or telephone (604) 736-2261 (The Province) or 736-2281 (The Sun).

"We're both also avid skiers and wanted to experience some different skiing while we were both young enough to enjoy it."

- Retired Idaho farmer living in Richmond

The Georgia Straight is an entertainment newspaper that comes out weekly. It can give you an idea of what's happening on an on-going basis in Vancouver and all over the Lower Mainland. Subscription rates are $20 per year. The address is 2110 West 4th Avenue, Vancouver, B.C. V6K 1N6.

There are many community-oriented weeklies and real estate papers that are worthwhile taking to give you valuable clues on community life. Their addresses are noted in the descriptions of individual neighborhoods below.

West End, Stanley Park in rush hour

Neighborhoods

Until the post-war development boom began for Vancouver, there were many private turn-of-the-century, two-storey family homes in what is now the city's downtown commercial and business district. As the development wave rolled across the city, those homes were pushed out by high-density, high-rise urban development, most of it commercial. One area, however, grew into a high-rise residential area, the West End, where population density is the highest in the country.

The West End

The West End is an attractive place for any urbanite on a number of counts. It is within walking distance of the city's core and all of its amenities. Yet its main streets, Denman and Robson, are also well-enough developed commercially that you don't need to enter the steel and glass canyons of downtown to obtain your daily living needs.

On the west side of this neighborhood is Stanley Park, a huge, forested area with recreation facilities such as lawn bowling, tennis and par-3 golf. There is a long sea-wall walk and a beach at English Bay, literally a stone's throw from many apartments. And there is a well-developed community centre and library on Denman.

Of course, the news can't be all good. There is also a well-developed nightlife on West End main streets. For some, that's part of the good news, but it also means some late night traffic noise and street people.

Housing in the West End can be extremely expensive. There is a mix here of rental apartments and condominiums. Some are in the same price range as similar accommodation elsewhere in the city but the demand is high, considering the West End's proximity to the downtown core, and finding them may involve some patience.

The community newspaper here is the The Westender, 1035 Davie Street, Vancouver, B.C., V6E 1M5. You can subscribe from another province for $35 for six months. This same firm also publishes the Eastender, covering community news east of Main Street right out to Burnaby.

False Creek

False Creek, a long inlet off English Bay, used to be the industrial adjunct to downtown Vancouver. The Canadian National Railway established its main rail yard and station here, along with sawmills and other manufacturing plants.

Today, False Creek's north shore is the site of Expo 86, Vancouver's world fair. On the south side is an imaginative housing development with two neighborhoods and a small park in between them. In the middle of it all is Granville Island Public Market, with theatres, shops and restaurants.

Housing prices on the south side range up and down the scale, depending on location, size and, in this case, view. The Expo site on the north side is slated for residential development, possibly the most ambitious in the history of Vancouver. Little is known of the proposed development at this writing, but it is expected to cover a wide range of housing styles and be available to a wide range of income groups.

South side, False Creek

Shaughnessy Heights

Shaughnessy was the first 'status' neighborhood in Vancouver, centred approximately on Granville Street as it runs south from the city, between Sixteenth and Thirty-Third streets.

Some of the old mansions are designated heritage sites, and a few of them house consulate offices of foreign countries. The lower end of the price scale here is around $300,000 and the rental housing, which consists of a limited number of luxury apartments, some in old mansions, is also quite pricey.

Kitsilano

From the south end of Burrard Street Bridge, west along the south shore of English Bay, 'Kits', as it is known to the locals, stretches out as a residential area with a density far below the high-rise West End but well above other predominantly single-family dwelling neighborhoods. That's because Kits is being gradually converted to an area of low-rise or duplex/fourplex apartment dwellings.

There is plenty of commercial development along the main street here, Broadway, but away from Broadway, development is almost exclusively residential. The Kits Beach on English Bay is closeby, and Vanier Park with its Planetarium and Museum are near the south end of Burrard Street Bridge.

Kitsilano is a popular place for the university community, where students can find a place to rent at a reasonable price, within cycling distance of the campus.

Point Grey/University Endowment Lands

Point Grey is one of the first residential neighborhoods to see huge homes on large lots. It is expensive, upper-middle to upper class living. Start thinking in terms of $300,000 and up, and add the cost of the gardener you'll need to maintain the property.

The University Endowment Lands are an extension of Point Grey. This large wooded area was given to the University of British Columbia in the 1920s to ensure it had room to expand. Some of the

House near UBC in University Endowment Lands

"I thought I wouldn't find Vancouver too much of a change because it's a big city, but I've found the people to be very different. No one has any time for me. I guess I just never noticed it in Montreal because I was busier, but I don't have any good friends here.
"It was really difficult to get to know anyone at first, and then when you do know them, they usually move away. I don't like Kerrisdale for that reason. It's so depressing. All these old people either die or move away. And it's expensive."

- Retired widow
in Vancouver

property has been sold for private residences as a way of raising money for UBC. The Endowment Lands are administered by the provincial government and policed by the RCMP, outside the municipal jurisdiction of the City of Vancouver. Homes here are very big, on very large lots and very expensive.

Kerrisdale

Kerrisdale is situated slightly south of Shaughnessy and is less expensive. But it is not cheap by any means because it is still mostly zoned single-family, in contrast to the multiple-family units of Kitsilano. Between Kerrisdale and Kitsilano, there are transition areas where the ratio of single to multiple family dwellings varies between these extremes.

Pockets of commercial development in Kerrisdale provide the amenities required by residents.

There are five golf courses in the immediate Kerrisdale/Point Grey area. Two of them - Point Grey Golf Course and Shaughnessy Golf and Country Club - are private. The other three - McCleery, Langara and University golf courses - are open to the public.

South and East Vancouver

The south and east areas of the city are predominated by single-family housing generally occupied by working class, middle-income families. Occasionally, there is a decided ethnic character to particular neighborhoods.

Housing here is generally less expensive and without a view. There are signs of increased residential construction activity in the future. The southern part of this area contains industrial development. And while there is a beautiful and expensive shopping mall at Oak and 41st Street, many of the local residents flee across the Knight Street Bridge to malls in Richmond.

Burnaby/ New Westminster

Thirty-five years ago, a drive to New Westminster, about 20 kilometres away along the main thoroughfare of Kingsway, was like a trip in the country. Today, it is solid development.

New Westminster and the Municipality of Burnaby saw the most rapid residential growth as bedroom communities for the Lower Mainland and as major blue-collar areas. Today, their own industrial and commercial development employs much of their resident workforces.

From Britain to British Columbia

Being British is no longer the advantage it once was if you are considering moving to British Columbia for your retirement.

Contrary to popular perceptions, British immigrants are subject to the same laws and regulations applicable to any prospective immigrant. Those requirements are detailed, as they relate primarily to American immigrants, on page 16.

Once you have applied for immigration, you should also apply for your British pension, if you are eligible, since a six-month wait for your first cheque is not uncommon.

British pensions are indexed, even for British citizens living in many countries abroad. But for Britains living in Canada, the pension is frozen at the level it was when they entered the country. The British Pensioners' Association sprang up here in Canada to lobby British Parliament for indexing of British pensions. This pensioners' group is also concerned about delays in receiving pensions, due primarily to delays in the mail.

There is a British Consulate office in Vancouver which can answer your specific questions on immigration to Canada from Britain. (Telephone (604) 683-4421)

New Westminster is the outer terminus of the new ALRT commuter train which can take you to downtown Vancouver in about 20 minutes. It is also the site of a major long-term redevelopment in its core urban area. Housing in New West is reasonably-priced and split evenly between apartment and single-family units.

Burnaby is more single-family unit oriented - mostly two- and three-bedroom bungalows, many 25 years old or more, but interspersed liberally with apartments and condominiums. There is no shortage of shopping and personal services and little need to venture into the metropolis for living necessities.

"We haven't met too many people outside of the seniors centre. Everyone seems to be off on their own here doing what they want to do."

East Vancouver off Kingsway

North and West Vancouver

Thirty years ago, Vancouver city residents looked north across Burrard Inlet to virgin forest. About 20 years ago, the area began growing rapidly as a residential suburb of the city and within 10 years, most of the trees were gone, replaced by what are now known as North and West Vancouver. As the housing developments moved higher up the North Shore mountain slopes, so did the prices. Spectacular views command spectacular prices. The two municipalities have become rather expensive bedroom communities.

Although it is a delightful and self-contained area, the north shore communities are linked to Vancouver by two bridges, the Lion's Gate and the Second Narrows, and in more recent years, by the Seabus commuter ferry. Morning and afternoon rush hours are a headache for thousands of Vancouver workers heading to work or home, but retired people can usually avoid rush hours.

West Vancouver is a little more quaint and a lot more expensive than North Vancouver. There are few bargains, either in private homes, condominiums or apartments.

Subscribing to the North Shore News will be helpful in considering North and West Vancouver. The paper comes out three times per week, but you can subscribe to just the Friday issue. It has a whole section devoted to real estate advertising as well as the local news. Taking just the Friday paper would cost $40 per year or $5 per month. Taking all three editions published each week would cost $55 for six months. The mailing address is 1139 Lonsdale Avenue, North Vancouver, B.C., V7M 2H4, telephone (604) 986-1337.

"We live kind of out of the way in North Vancouver because we wanted it that way. We've never had much time for ourselves so now is it."

"I rent an apartment in the city of North Vancouver and since I'm by myself, I go to the seniors centre whenever I can. It helps pass the time."

"North Vancouver seems to be true 'west coast' to us. We have a house which we consider to be very 'west coast' - glass and cedar."

Richmond/Surrey/Delta

"Well, that Steveston centre has a museum and everything, you know. It's a pretty good place to meet people."

"Richmond is good for us because it has everything we need - recreation, medical services, shopping malls, and it's close to Vancouver without being too busy."

These three municipalities lie to the south of Vancouver and have been predominantly agricultural, taking advantage of the rich flood plain deposits of the Fraser River delta.

Richmond has since become the most urban of the three, with a population of about 110,000 living primarily on Lulu Island in the Fraser River delta. Sea Island is also in the municipality but it is the site of Vancouver International Airport. Because of the airport, hotels and an abundance of good restaurants have sprung up in Richmond. There are three major shopping mall developments - Lansdowne Park, Richmond Square and Richmond Centre - where major department stores and all the personal ser-

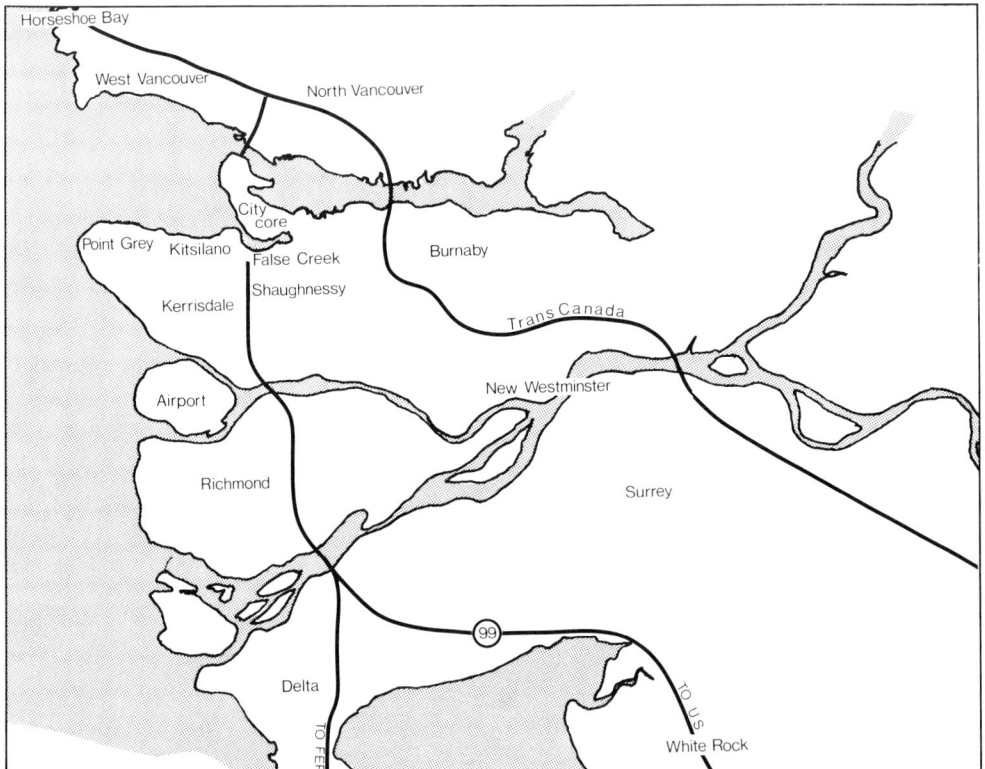

vices you would ever need are represented.

Surrey and Delta are more rural in character than Richmond, though there are pockets of residential and commercial development scattered throughout. Housing is generally quite affordable here. There are plenty of larger pieces of property available and a number of housing developments for retired people.

There are a number of newspapers publishing in this area, among them the Surrey Leader, Box 276, Surrey, B.C., V3T 4W8, the North Delta Sentinel, 10680 - 84th Avenue, Delta, B.C., V4C 2L2, The Richmond News, 118-3633 Third Avenue, Richmond, B.C., V6X 2B9, the Richmond Review, 5811-A Cedarbridge Way, Richmond, B.C., V6X 2A8, and the Delta Optimist, 5020 48th Street, Delta, B.C., V4K 3N5.

"We both have always liked the parts of Canada we've been. We wanted to get away from the cold and live in an urban centre. That's why we like Richmond. It's close enough to Vancouver but also far enough away that we don't get wrapped up in city life."

- Retired Idaho farmer

"Well, I golf a lot and we like a big city and the wife here likes to shop, so I golf here in Richmond (there are half a dozen or so places to golf) and Myrna shops.

White Rock's white rock

White Rock

S tatistics for White Rock could easily convince you it is the ideal retirement community of British Columbia.

It is a city of 15,000, ideally-located on the warm waters of Semiahmoo Bay with several kilometres of sandy beach front. The sun shines an average of almost 2,000 hours each year here and it has the lowest annual rainfall of the Vancouver-Lower Mainland area - about 109 cm.

Almost 34 per cent of its population is 55 years or older. Its 7,000 households take up 55 per cent of the usable land within the city, while only eight per cent is used by commercial and industrial buildings.

White Rock extends east and west along the bay for a distance of only five kilometres. Its northern border with the sprawling municipality of Surrey is only a kilometre from the waterfront. It is about 50 kilometres south of Vancouver on the four-lane freeway Highway 99 and only 32 kilometres from Vancouver International Airport and the B.C. Ferry terminal at Tsawwassen.

White Rock gets its name from a huge white rock located at the eastern end of the beach. There are as many legends about its origins as there are people to tell them. Most of them spring from coast Indian folklore.

On any given summer Saturday and Sunday, the casual viewer might think the entire population of Vancouver is lying on White Rock's beaches, soaking up the sun, or jamming its popular promenade along Beach Drive. Come October, White Rock reverts to a delightful, and quiet, little city on the sea.

White Rock is small: it is easy to move around here without having to rely on major transportation services. There are many seniors facilities and services yet White Rock is within easy reach of metropolitan

"We chose White Rock because the weather is a little better than Vancouver. We used to rent an apartment in Kitsilano but it was too busy all year long - tourists in the summer and students in the winter. White Rock is nice and quiet in the wintertime."

Vancouver and all of its amenities. The only inconvenience appears to be coping with the summer influx of visitors.

Housing

Because it is an old, established community, and a long-time summer resort area, there is a unique mix of housing. Many of the existing homes were originally summer beach houses, renovated to become year-round residences. Its slow development is reflected in the varied architectural styles, from 1920s summer cottages to 1980s contemporary.

The average two- or three-bedroom home sells in the $75,000 to $80,000 range. But prices can range up and down the scale from there.

White Rock has its share of apartments. There are also three fairly large, modern, condominium developments. Two of them cater to adults and seniors only. The third is a retirement home.

There are no cooperative housing developments in White Rock, but there are a number in neighboring Surrey. Further information on housing cooperatives in that area and the whole of the Lower Mainland, can be obtained from Shirley Green, Columbia Housing Cooperative Association, telephone 255-7733.

Medical Services

White Rock has several doctors, dentists and clinics. Peace Arch District Hospital is located in the downtown White Rock area, directly across from the City Hall.

There is no shortage of drug stores and pharmacies in the downtown area and in the several shopping centres that surround the community.

"White Rock appeals to us because it's small. If we need medical attention, there's the Surrey hospital not far away, so we're not lacking anything essential."

Shopping and Transportation

White Rock is a complete community as far as shopping and personal services are concerned. In the city itself, shopping is a simple matter and can be done easily on foot. There are a number of shopping centres. One of them, Semiahmoo Centre, contains more than 70 retail outlets and services. The area has its share of small corner grocery and convenience stores.

The city and neighboring Surrey are served by re-

"We only live here in the winter, so we have a condominium that has a security system. We go back to Saskatchewan for the summer to be with friends."

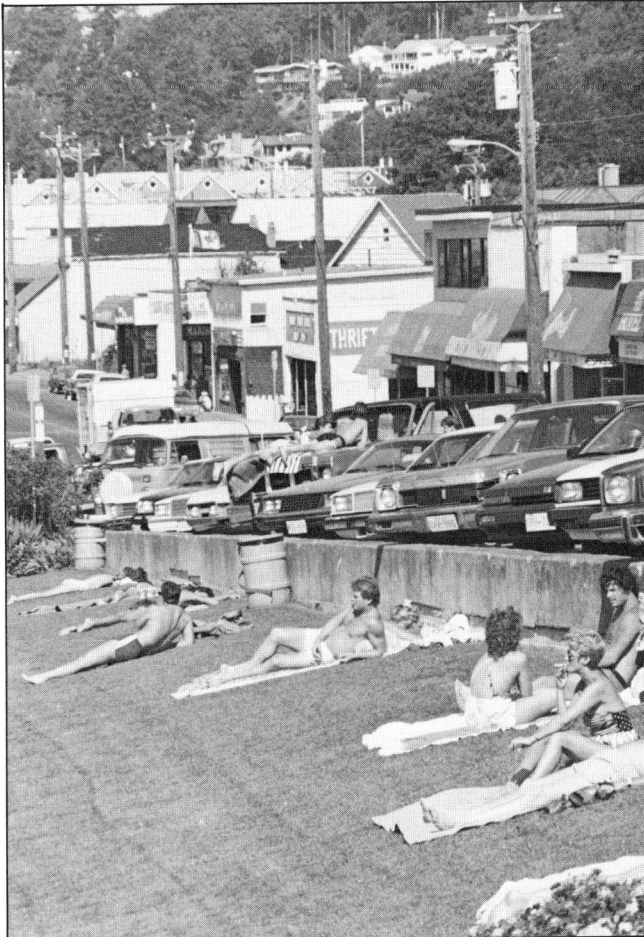

Beach Drive in White Rock

gional buses that takes riders into downtown Vancouver. The new Skytrain elevated commuter train can be boarded in New Westminster heading for downtown Vancouver. Buses from White Rock connect with the ALRT in New Westminster. A car is not essential but it is most certainly a convenience for travelling away from the city.

Recreation, Entertainment, News, Radio and TV

"Yes, we go to the seniors centre to visit with friends. It's a central location for us."

There is considerable opportunity for recreation designed for seniors in the White Rock city area. The Senior Citizens Activity Centre is located downtown, close to City Hall. As well, there is a Seniors'

Medical Services for Short-

Retirement years inevitably bring with them infirmities and conditions that lie somewhere between complete health and illness requiring acute medical care. For example, you may develop a condition that needs monitoring, or require supervision in recovering from some surgery.

In British Columbia, there are a variety of services outside the acute care system that address just such needs.

Adult day centres are operated by non-profit organizations and volunteers for those who might otherwise be homebound. In addition to health services, such as therapy or exercise, they offer social activities, including day trips, arts and crafts, music and lunch.

In addition, there are several at-home services, which vary according to your treatment requirements.

Drop-in Centre, with transportation to and from provided. There are two other senior citizens organizations in the city: Canadian National Pensioners, and the Old Age Pensioners.

Within a short distance of the city, there are three golf courses and the White Rock-South Surrey Swimming Pool, where hours are set aside for seniors' social swims. White Rock also has a well-stocked library and a small but well-patronized art gallery.

Term Needs

Home maker services provide relief for the care giver. A home maker is placed in the home for one or several days, depending on the need. If necessary, the person needing care may be placed in a care facility for several weeks to allow the care giver a longer rest. You can contact the local health unit office in each community for information.

Also included in at-home services is home care nursing, for those who require more extensive care such as administering medications, changing dressings, or monitoring a condition. Charges for these services are based upon your taxable income. If you paid no taxes in the previous year, there is no charge for these services.

Meals on Wheels provides a hot meal for homebound patients. The cost for the service at this writing varies between $2.50 and $3.45 depending on the type of meal you order.

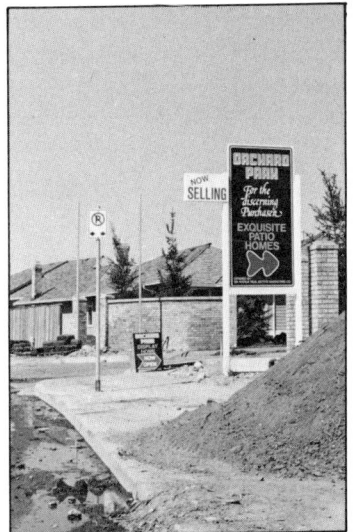

A common site in White Rock, enclave communities

Victoria's Inner Harbor

Victoria

Of all of British Columbia's cities, Victoria is the favorite retirement centre. It's a pretty city. Despite a busy downtown business core, Victoria leaves the impression of being more a large village than a metropolitan area. There is good reason for that. Victoria is considerably smaller than Vancouver.

The City of Victoria is actually just a small part of a cluster of communities known as Greater Victoria. These communities include the core municipalities of Saanich, Oak Bay and Esquimalt, the rural municipalities of Central and North Saanich, the Village of Sidney and the 'western communities' of View Royal, Colwood, Langford and Metchosin. Total population of Greater Victoria is about 225,000.

The outlying and more rural community of Sooke to the west is not generally considered part of Greater Victoria. (From here on, we will use the term "Victoria" to mean Greater Victoria and "City of Victoria" to mean just that municipality.)

Victoria is almost non-industrial. Most of its original industries have long since fled to the Lower Mainland.

The major employers in the city today are the provincial government, the naval base in Esquimalt, the tourism and convention industry. Victoria is also the home port of a large part of the Pacific fishing fleet. In addition, some farming is done on the Saanich Peninsula.

There's a tangible sense of community in Victoria. You can see it in the extra touches it gives to the downtown atmosphere - its hanging flower baskets and its downtown redevelopment program that has seen, among other improvements, removal of all overhead wiring. Victorians are conscious of the city's place in the history of the province. There are tax incentives for private owners to restore heritage homes and buildings to their original grandeur. From

"I really enjoy gardening. . . it's therapeutic for me. I use the university a lot. I use it more for reading and going to the school of music concerts."

- retired Ottawa civil servant
now living in Victoria

time to time, these restored homes are open to the public and it is generally the locals, not the tourists, who are interested.

Victoria is a friendly place to live. The city has a number of well-defined neighborhoods. The two most popular, and indicative of the Victoria lifestyle, are James Bay and Fairfield. Outside the City of Victoria, Oak Bay, Esquimalt and Saanich seem to be large neighborhoods of the city even though they are separate municipalities. Beyond that, some 30 kilometres north of the city near the Swartz Bay ferry terminal, lies Sidney, a village that is attracting increasing numbers of retired people with its easy, non-city lifestyle.

All of these areas, of course, share the same kind of weather and other characteristics. Those features they have in common will be discussed in this general section on Victoria. Unique aspects of these neighborhoods will be described later in this section.

Weather

Because of its mild, damp climate, Victoria proclaims itself Canada's City of Gardens. It rains, on average, 138 days a year here. The annual average temperature is 10 degrees Celsius, ranging from a winter average of 4.1 degrees to a summer average of 16 degrees. There is usually a breeze, even on the hottest of days.

Spring arrives a little earlier in Victoria than in other areas of Canada. Crocuses, daffodils and tulips blossom here before the snow has melted in many Canadian cities.

During the winter months, clouds are a fact of life. Rain is not as frequent nor as heavy as in Vancouver but, for the newcomer, rain gear is usually on the shopping list.

Because of its ocean surroundings, Victoria experiences a unique weather phenomenon. It can be raining in one part of Greater Victoria while the sun is shining in another. Thunderstorms are rare.

Dallas Road in storm

Victoria has had snow each year for the past six. It is normally very wet and gone in less than a week but has been known to persist for as much as a month.

"Victoria is a nice city, but the damp weather isn't good for my health.

- 92 year old southern Alberta school teacher

Housing

As in any Canadian city of similar size, home prices cover a wide range. At this writing, average single-family, two- and three-bedroom homes sell for between $75,000 and $90,000. Depending on size, age and location, homes can drop as low as $50,000 and soar in excess of $1 million.

Apartment buildings are scattered throughout Victoria. A bylaw now limits them to four storeys within the city of Victoria but there are a few highrises.

Apartment rents average from $350 to $500 monthly but be prepared to pay much more for choice locations. For example, waterfront properties and those with a view command higher-than-average prices.

Most apartments are one- or two-bedrooms. In newer buildings, they usually have a small entrance, hall, small kitchen, bathroom, large living-dining area, reasonably-large bedrooms and outside balcony.

Older apartment blocks, generally located in or very close to the downtown core, are usually roomier but rarely feature an outside balcony.

Medical Services

Victoria and its surrounding areas are well-served by a variety of hospitals.

Victoria General Hospital, a few miles from the downtown area, was built only recently and is the most modern of the acute care facilities.

Royal Jubilee Hospital is a sprawling conglomeration of older buildings in Oak Bay but close to Victoria's city centre.

Saanich Peninsula Hospital serves the large area north of Victoria to Sidney.

All three hospitals have emergency wards.

There is a large medical community, ample nursing services and an excellent ambulance service.

Shopping and Transportation

Victoria's downtown core provides a variety of retail outlets from the small exclusive boutiques to national department stores. All major banks and trust companies are represented, and the majority of Greater Victoria's medical, dental and legal services are found in the downtown area.

Shopping in the downtown core can be done quite comfortably on foot because of the area's compact layout. Located in the downtown district are Hudson's Bay and Eaton's.

The main shopping street, Government, has the atmosphere of an outdoor mall as it is designed to carry much less traffic than the other main thoroughfares in the area, Douglas and Wharf.

Much work has been done to preserve an historic character to the downtown area of Victoria, and on that count alone, it is a pleasant place to stroll. The Chinese community has also done much to restore and beautify what is left of the original Chinatown, at one time the largest on the Pacific coast.

Outside of the downtown core are three large shopping centres, none more than a 10-minute drive away. Hillside Shopping Centre contains a large Sears department store. Mayfair is the home of Woodward's department store and a second Eaton's store is located in the Tillicum Shopping Mall.

The neighborhoods outside the downtown area contain a number of smaller shopping centres and a good selection of small corner grocery and convenience stores supplying daily shopping essentials.

A provincially-sponsored Meals on Wheels program provides hot meals to persons who cannot cook or go out for meals. Most seniors activity centres also provide a food service at a nominal cost.

Because Victoria is on an island, some retail prices will be higher than in Lower Mainland communities due to transportation costs.

With the exception of heating oil, which is the most common fuel for heating homes, most monthly expenses are fairly stable. Oil, like gasoline, fluctuates with world market prices.

Bus transportation in the Greater Victoria area is provided by the Capital Regional Transit System. During the morning and afternoon rush periods, service is frequent. In outlying areas, service is less frequent and bus stops are farther apart.

There is no shortage of sea and air transport to and from the island. The most heavily-used is the B.C. Ferry system from Swartz Bay, about 32 kilometres north of Victoria. These very large ferries serve both the Lower Mainland and the Gulf Islands. Bus service via ferry can take you from downtown Victoria to downtown Vancouver in about three hours.

Victoria's International Airport provides frequent air service both to Vancouver and cities in Washington state. A float plane service also operates between Victoria's Inner Harbor and Vancouver harbor.

From Victoria's Inner Harbor, there are three sailings daily to Port Angeles in Washington during the summer months on Black Ball Ferry's vessel, Coho. This is reduced to once daily in the fall and winter. The trip takes one hour.

During the summer months, the ocean-going steamship, Princess Marguerite, once owned by the CPR and now operated by the Crown corporation B.C. Steamships, travels once daily between Victoria and Seattle. It's a five-hour trip.

"Victoria is fine. I couldn't move anywhere now, even if I wanted to. I spend quite a bit of time downtown, doing my shopping, since it's handy."

- Woman, retired from Winnipeg 20 years ago

Government Street shopping

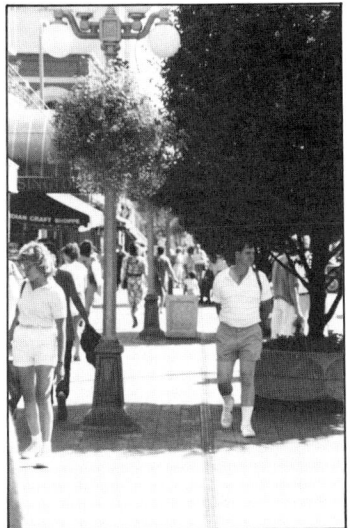

"You should go see that Oak Bay Lodge. It's just beautiful. It was supposed to be a hotel, you know."

Recreation, Entertainment, News, Radio and TV

There are plenty of recreational and entertainment possibilities for any age group in Victoria. For example, there are five movie houses in Victoria with a total of 13 cinemas. Two theatres, the MacPherson

Is your will moving?

It doesn't take a psychologist to observe that people are usually reluctant to confront the prospect of diminishing mental capacity and eventual mortality.

But a lawyer will tell you that failure to address these issues creates most of the legal problems that older people and their families have to confront. As you plan your retirement, you do have an opportunity to come to grips with them.

How many times in the past 10 or 20 years have you thought, 'I must get the wills out of the safety deposit box and see if they're still okay.' If you are considering relocating for your retirement years, there's no better time to consider the following:

1. Is my old will drafted so as to ensure a trouble-free administration under British Columbia law? While the laws are largely similar, except for Quebec, the courts of different provinces may treat issues such as one's obligations for spouses, children and other dependents, or the interpretation of particular words and phrases, in a different fashion. Have a lawyer review your will from this perspective. This will also give you an opportunity to establish a contact with a professional advisor before any crisis arises.

2. Have my spouse and I adequately planned for the possibility that we might both be killed in a joint disaster? Statistics show people travel

and the Royal, host live performances and there are a number of thriving theatre groups that make use of them. Prices are not outrageous to begin with and seniors can usually get discounts.

Of course, Victoria is also a city that attracts tourists with a number of worthwhile museums and even a castle, Craigdarroch, that has been restored to its original splendor. Butchart Gardens is not far away in Brentwood Bay.

Victoria is a city that is well-stocked with a diversity

"We've made a lot of really close friends out here. We travel a lot and we both enjoy golfing and gardening, which is something we both can enjoy 12 months a year in Victoria."

- Retired couple in
Colwood near Victoria

with you?

more in retirement. That increases the chance of such a disaster. If it happens and it is impossible to tell which of two people died first, the younger is presumed to have survived the older. In a typical husband and wife situation, all of the assets would then pass through the will of the younger spouse. This can create an unintended result if the husband and wife wanted to have different beneficiaries.

3. How appropriate and realistic is your choice of executor in light of your move? Will your spouse need the assistance of a professional executor, such as a trust company or qualified lawyer, if you are relocating in a new jurisdiction? How appropriate is your choice of an alternate executor if your spouse dies before you? Remember, your children may now be several thousands of miles away and may not be the logical choice for a smooth and convenient administration.

4. Now that your children may be grown and on their own, does your will adequately provide for their children if one of your children dies before you do? If you are close to your grandchildren, would you now want to consider a modest legacy for each grandchild?

Dust off your old will and take a realistic look at these and other issues. Then you'll really be able to relax.

Kite flying on Clover Point

"We're not really enjoying our retirement. It really wasn't what we expected. It's so difficult to meet people and we're quite lonely."

- Oak Bay resident

of restaurants. Take your pick - French, East Indian, Chinese, Italian, Mideastern - and there is a restaurant that will serve it up.

Golf and lawn bowling rank high on the list of outdoor recreation for seniors, mainly because the climate allows play for most of the year. There are 11 golf courses in the Greater Victoria area, five of them open to the public at any time, another four that are semi-private and two that are private. There is normally a waiting list for membership in these clubs. There are at least two lawn bowling clubs, one in Oak Bay and the other at Beacon Hill Park. Both accept new members in the spring.

There are several municipally or regionally operated recreation centres that usually combine a swimming pool, curling or skating rink, tennis courts and a combination of other smaller facilities. Most have whirlpools and steam baths, and one, the Oak Bay Recreation Centre, even has an indoor waterslide. (And yes, it is also well-used by retired, but not retiring, seniors)

These recreation centres have organized exercise and activity programs designed to appeal to retired people and in some cases, such as the Oak Bay, the seniors programming rivals other programming in its size and scope.

For the fisherman, Victoria is paradise. There are many marinas where one can moor a boat permanently and plenty of boat launch opportunities if you want to take the boat home at night. Salt water fishing among the protected islands of Haro and Georgia Straits will be a treat for prairie puddle fishers.

Seniors activity and recreation centres abound in the Greater Victoria area. Many are funded by the federal New Horizons program. Others are supported by churches or service clubs.

Many activity centres feature specially-priced tours to other parts of Canada, the United States or overseas.

The city is home to all of the major service clubs found in any North American city. Branches of most of those clubs will be found in the surrounding municipalities. There is also a wide variety of other clubs, such as garden and flower clubs, kennel clubs, cat and horse fancier clubs, public speaking clubs and music clubs.

Camosun College and the University of Victoria offer wide ranging programs of extension, credit and night school courses. Some courses are offered at no charge or nominal charge to seniors.

Victoria has one daily newspaper, the Times-Colonist. Also available for daily home delivery are the Vancouver Sun, The Province and the Toronto Globe and Mail. There are also a number of community weekly newspapers, many delivered to the door free of charge.

There are four local radio stations: CJVI, CKDA, CFAX and CFMS-FM. Some stations in Vancouver and the Seattle area are also available, with or without cable service.

There are two local television stations. CHEK-TV is part of the national CTV network, with some local news broadcasting. Channel 10 is a community sta-

Breakwater at Ogden Point in James Bay

tion, featuring only local events and activities.

The area is served by cable television, delivering 11 Canadian and American stations. An even wider variety of broadcasting is available with a converter on commercial-free pay television.

Neighborhoods

Fairfield

Fairfield spreads east from downtown Victoria, bounded by Beacon Hill Park - the city's largest and most beautiful - on its west, the Municipality of Oak Bay on its east and Cook Street on the west. Fairfield Road is its main east-west thoroughfare. Most of Fairfield, with the exception of the Cook Street area, is more than a pleasant walk to downtown. Public transit is available, but a car would be handy.

Fairfield is the largest residential area within the City of Victoria and attracts a diverse mix of people, housing and residential amenities.

Single-family homes, children, household pets and well-tended gardens are the hallmark of Fairfield. In recent years, there has been an apartment development program as older homes fell to the wrecker.

The apartment population is, for the most part, composed of young childless couples, singles and retired people. Its private home occupants are generally well-established families or older couples whose families have left, but who have not yet surrendered to the need to sell the house and live in a less demanding residence.

Homes range from the substantial early 1920's design to contemporary. Many of the large homes have been converted into apartment residences. They are popular with retired people because of their more "homey" atmosphere, their location, and usually their lower rents.

The average price of private homes and condominiums is in the $80,000 to $90,000 range, varying

Best place to shop
- Fairfield Plaza

Best place to go for a walk
- Beacon Hill Park

Best place to get groceries
- Shop Easy on Cook Street

Best teahouse (restaurant)
- Tudor Rose Tearoom on Cook Street

Best coffee and doughnuts
- Ian's coffee shop

Best bakery
- Captain Cooks on Fort Street

Best dry cleaners
- One-Hour Martinizing on Cook Street

Best place to meet people
- Fairfield New Horizon's Centre

Best garage
- Fairfield Shell Service

Best medical centre
- Fairfield Health Centre

with age, size and location. Monthly apartment rents average $350 to $500, again depending on age and location.

The population of Fairfield is as diverse as its housing, a mix of white and blue collar workers, established families and young married couples with their eyes on moving to "something better."

Its large retired population is attracted there by reasonable housing prices, its proximity to downtown Victoria and the ease of community shopping. The scenic waterfront is also a factor.

Fairfield has no central commercial core as do James Bay and neighboring Oak Bay Municipality. It is a widespread, strictly residential area.

Because of its gradual growth over the last 80 or so years, Fairfield has no run-down areas. As homes

"We like Fairfield because it has such different people - young hippies, couples, families, and elderly people."

- retired Fairfield resident

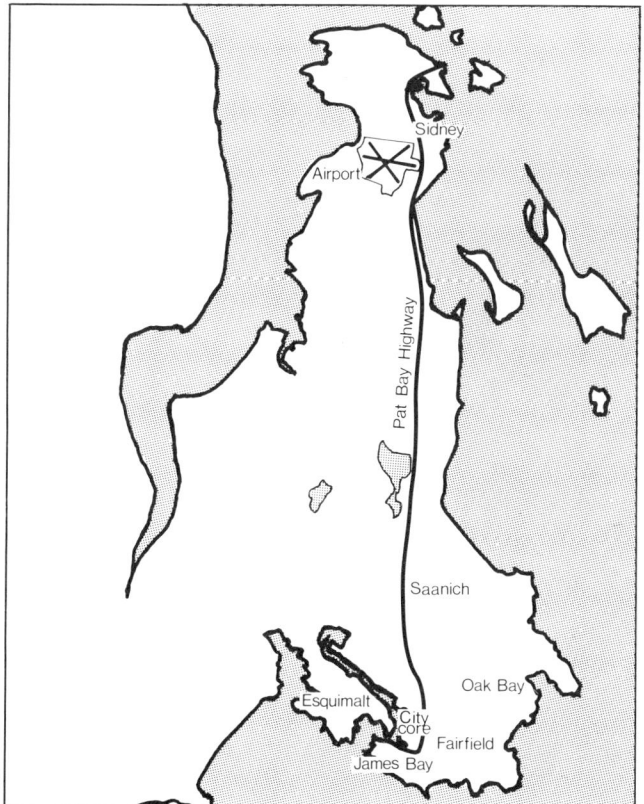

and buildings became obsolete, they were torn down and replaced with newer structures. It has a nice mix of housing, old and new, large and small.

There is only one shopping mall in the area, located on Fairfield Road at about the geographical centre of the community. Another shopping area, on tree-lined lower Cook Street a few blocks from Dallas Road, has the atmosphere of a small village unto itself, with a large food market and a variety of smaller stores. Few places in Fairfield are far from the nearest corner or convenience store.

Not far from the Fairfield Road shopping mall is a busy, well-patronized New Horizons seniors' activity centre. A community centre operates volunteer services, but the community has no major recreation facility. Closeby, however, is the Oak Bay Recreation Centre, one of the best in the Greater Victoria area.

James Bay

Best hairdresser
- Renee's Hair Studio
or James Bay Beauty Salon

Best shopping
- James Bay Shopping Centre

Best bakery
- Golden Sheaf on Fort Street

Best restaurant
- James Bay Tearoom

James Bay is an historic neighborhood that has much to recommend it as a retirement community.

It is close enough to the downtown business community to be reached in a comfortable 15-minute walk. It is almost self-sustaining with a compact and complete shopping centre at the hub of the community.

There is an interesting mix of housing and people: a high proportion of retired people, living side by side with young marrieds, single parents and children.

Housing ranges from old, well-preserved single-family homes to modern high-rise condominiums and apartments.

James Bay is a stroller's delight, with enviable waterfront scenery, pleasant beaches and acres of parkland.

The waterfront, however, can also be the scene of some pretty wild seasonal storms, with water splashing up so badly sometimes, that Dallas Road along the water has to be closed for safety.

James Bay is a relatively small area. That, combined with its historic significance, gives a sense of community to its residents, even the relative newcomers. The provincial legislative buildings are in this area. And painter Emily Carr once lived here.

Most James Bay streets are lined with spring blooming trees of the Prunus variety. It has its industry also, with marine-associated businesses fronting on the Inner Harbor. The Coast Guard has its major facility here. But for the most part, James Bay is an attractive mix of 'old but restored' or 'new and sometimes innovative' housing.

Private homes here average about $90,000 but waterfront locations command a premium. Condominium prices average about $100,000 in the higher ones with a view. Smaller, four-storey buildings and townhouses bring less. Monthly rents in apartments average from $350 to $400.

Popular among retired people in James Bay is the New Horizons activity centre and the James Bay shopping complex. The centre organizes a wide variety of activities from concerts to organized tours. The James Bay Community Centre, a few blocks away, is active in organizing a variety of community-oriented events for seniors.

Oak Bay

Victoria residents like to joke that residents of the Municipality of Oak Bay live behind the "Tweed Curtain" - a good-natured reference to the perception that a lot of retired English people live there.

The perception is exaggerated but the municipality capitalizes on the image. Its main shopping area is known as "the village." The annual summer outdoor fair, the Oak Bay Tea Party, features a parade, costumes, decor and food with a turn-of-the century English flavor.

With the exception of a few small shopping centres, and a very popular visitor attraction on Beach Drive called Oak Bay Marina, Oak Bay is a non-

"We don't get out too much. We don't have a car and find the transit system inadequate. We feel quite isolated."

- Retired Oak Bay resident

Best restaurant
- Blethering Place Tearoom

Best hairdresser
- Margo Beauty Salon at Hillside

Best shopping
- Monterey Mews

Best retirement centre
- The Oak Bay Lodge

Best seniors activities
- Oak Bay Rec Centre and Oak Bay Senior's Activity Centre

Best bakery
- Irene's bakery on Oak Bay Avenue

Best garage
- Oak Bay Automotive Ltd.

Best place to walk
- along the waterfront by the Oak Bay Marina

Best dry cleaners
- Individual Dry Cleaners on Fort

Best place to meet people
- Oak Bay Lawn Bowling Club

commercial, middle-class to wealthy residential community.

The most striking first impressions are its well-kept boulevards, tree-lined streets and its private gardens.

The municipality does have a high percentage of retired people and the "village" atmosphere has seemed to rub off on many of them.

With the exception of the Uplands area, most homes are one storey with two to four bedrooms. Oak Bay has its share of large older homes, high-rise waterfront apartments, condominiums and town houses.

The Uplands is another matter. It is very exclusive and very expensive. Most of the homes range upward from $200,000. There are no apartments, and no commercial development at all.

Oak Bay is bounded on the south and east by the sea, on the west by the City of Victoria and on the north by the Municipality of Saanich. The many beaches are pleasant and the views across the Juan

Shops in Oak Bay village

de Fuca Straits to the American Olympic Mountains, spectacular. But, as with James Bay, that waterfront can produce high winds and heavy seas during the storm seasons.

Oak Bay is the favored area of Greater Victoria as a retirement community but it's more expensive than most others.

Average private home prices in Oak Bay are in excess of $100,000. Waterfront properties and properties close to the Uplands run much higher than that.

Apartment block density is well below the rest of Greater Victoria but rents away from the waterfront are about the same. Waterfront apartments range above $1,000 per month.

There are many large, well-built, older homes in Oak Bay, designed originally to accommodate single families, and household staff. Today, for economic reasons, many of them have been converted into apartment residences. There are some still available as private homes, but they are costly to buy and costlier to maintain.

Oak Bay has always had many small corner stores and variety stores. But over the years, many of them have expanded into small shopping areas.

Its main shopping areas are located along Oak Bay Avenue, the major east-west connector to downtown Victoria. Oak Bay Village is at the eastern end of Oak Bay Avenue. There are a variety of food, clothing, drugs and hardware stores, as well as banking services, doctors' and dental offices and restaurants. Also located in the village area is the Oak Bay Municipal Hall. From anywhere in Oak Bay to downtown Victoria is a good 10 to 15 minutes by car or bus.

Oak Bay has one of the newest, largest and busiest community recreation centres in Greater Victoria. It contains an Olympic-sized swimming pool and skating rink, indoor tennis courts, a fitness centre, tanning studio, computer training centre and a large, licensed lounge that also serves meals and provides entertainment.

"That Blethering Place has the best raisin scones and they're very reasonable."

Aware of the retired population's needs, the recreation centre offers almost as many athletic and social programs for seniors as it does for the remainder of the community.

There is also a popular, and well-patronized, seniors activity centre just a few blocks away. It is a popular gathering place for retired residents and offers a wide variety of activities and entertainment.

The municipality is well-supplied with small, well-landscaped parks. There are parks for strolling and sitting or for athletics including a popular and busy

You've Found the District,

Once you've found the district where you want to live, should you buy or rent? You'll find a wide variety of options, ranging from the traditional single-family house to the time-shared, fully-serviced apartment complex. Increasing numbers of apartment buildings are now aimed directly at the seniors market and are designed to meet their needs, including food and medical services. These units can run to $3,000 per month but in that price range, the landlord will provide you with a limousine to take you to appointments.

If you'd like to become involved quickly in a group activity, co-operatives may be the way you should go.

There are now almost 200 cooperative housing projects in operation in British Columbia, with more on the way.

The idea behind cooperative housing is to provide affordable housing for everyone, regardless of financial resources and, at the same time, provide a sense of ownership to people who might not otherwise be able to afford private homes.

Anyone can become a member of a housing cooperative. All that is required is the price of a share, usually between $1,500 and $3,000. Monthly fees, or rent, on individual units are tied to tenant income. Even the highest rents charged fall below market rents.

lawn bowling club.

Besides the newspaper, radio and television services of Greater Victoria, Oak Bay has its own weekly community newspaper, the Oak Bay Star. For a subscription, address your letter to 202B - 2046 Oak Bay Avenue, Victoria, V8R 1E4.

Saanich

Saanich, like Oak Bay, is a municipality separate from the City of Victoria, with its own council, police

Where's the House?

A coop is governed by a council of elected tenants responsible for making and enforcing the rules of the development. The council also sets up committees to take care of complaints, maintenance, landscaping, repairs and tenant membership.

Because of the popularity of cooperative housing, there is always a waiting list. When someone moves out, the membership committee reviews the waiting list and selects a replacement.

This can give rise to problems. Vacancies occur most often among the higher income tenants because they are most able to move into the open housing market. To maintain a financial balance in the coop, the membership committee will then seek a tenant who can afford the same rent scale as the departing tenant. That often means bypassing lower income members. Some bitterness often results.

Condominiums require the same commitment to manage the affairs of the building but provide a more marketable asset. There is usually no grass to cut and no garden to tend.

You should consider whether the other owners are compatible, what proportion of the units are occupied and if you have sufficient resources beyond the expected costs to take care of the unexpected costs that face all major projects.

and fire service. It extends north from Victoria along the Saanich Peninsula towards the Village of Sidney. Between it and Sidney are two more municipalities, Central and North Saanich.

Saanich is still developing at a rapid pace but, as yet, there is little overall sense of community among its residents. Rather, there is a feeling of local community in the developed areas. It is a family municipality with plenty of children and pets.

Until the end of World War II, virtually the whole of the peninsula was farmland. Following the war, the demand for housing spread north from Victoria, turning Saanich into a large bedroom municipality.

Large parts of Saanich are rural with pockets of housing development in between. There are many hobby farms, often owned and operated by people who have another job during the week and become farmer/ranchers on weekends and evenings.

Home prices vary widely in the three Saanich Peninsula municipalities. Besides location and the other usual price factors, municipal services to the house or lot also make a difference and should be taken note of. Many parts of the municipality are still without sidewalks. Streetlighting is sparse or non-existent in many districts and many homes are still serviced by septic field.

Homes built in the last 30 years average between $70,000 and $90,000. Prices of older homes range widely outside of those figures depending on location, services available and the amount of land they occupy.

There is limited apartment and condominium development. Waterfront property commands a premium, as usual.

Slightly lower real estate prices in Saanich make it attractive to the home buyer. But along with lower prices go fewer municipal services, substantial travelling time to Victoria and the need for private transportation.

Though it is served by the regional transit system, a car is essential. Bus service is sparse during most of the day, and the nearest bus stop can be many blocks away.

Saanich itself has no central core but rather a number of shopping centre developments that have grown up alongside the many housing developments, large and small. There are also many individual small neighborhood stores selling groceries and a variety of other household needs.

While there is no major recreation complex like the Oak Bay Recreation Centre in Saanich municipality, there is one up the Saanich Peninsula near Sidney, the Panorama Leisure Centre. The centre has a 25-metre pool, an ice arena, tennis courts, fitness classes, 'rehab' swims and a variety of classes specifically for seniors. There is a New Horizons activity centre and, in and around Saanich, several golf courses, including:

☐ the 18-hole Uplands Golf Club in neighboring Oak Bay adjacent to the expensive Uplands residential district (membership fees to this private course are up to $5,000 plus annual dues of about $600),

☐ Cedar Hill Golf Club, an 18-hole public course nestled in a middle-class residential neighborhood on Saanich's border with the city,

☐ Gorge Vale Golf Club, a semi-private 18-hole course in nearby Esquimalt.

☐ Royal Oak Inn Golf Club, a private 9-hole course near Beaver Lake Park associated with the Royal Oak Inn or

☐ Nine-hole courses located at Prospect Lake, Henderson Park (par 3) and Mount Douglas (par 3).

In one sense, Saanich is very much a rural community. Friendships are struck up easily with neighbors in the many housing developments much as they are in small towns. Yet it is part of a large urban community.

The community newspaper that serves most of the Saanich Peninsula is the Sidney Review. You can subscribe by writing The Review, P.O. Box 2070, Sidney, B.C., V8L 3S5.

Sidney

The Village of Sidney is located at the northern tip of the Saanich Peninsula, about 32 kilometres from Victoria. The main road to Victoria, Highway 17, the Patricia Bay Highway, gets you to downtown Victoria in about 30 minutes.

In recent years, Sidney has become a favorite residential area for thousands of people who work in Greater Victoria and who are willing to trade off commuting for lower housing costs.

For that reason, Sidney has enjoyed something of a building boom.

Sidney is a friendly place with a comfortable, small-town atmosphere: a village in the true sense. Its retail centre is compact, offering all of the essential services. It is primarily residential with some light, marine-oriented industry. It is the British Columbia terminus of the Washington State ferry service to Anacortes and is located just a few minutes drive from both the B.C. Ferry terminal at Swartz Bay and Victoria's International Airport.

Sidney is adjacent to excellent salmon fishing waters. Its many marinas house hundreds of private boats of all sizes, more often than not, owned by people who don't live in Sidney. Summer weekends are usually busy in the village.

Sidney Spit Provincial Marine Park lies a short way offshore. It is accessible only by boat and attracts scores of boaters from Washington State as well as the Greater Victoria area.

Because of its sheltered location, Sidney is spared some of the severe seasonal storms that lash the Victoria waterfront areas.

With Victoria's International Airport just across the highway, jetliners pass over the community at low altitude, creating some noise problems.

Most of the housing construction in the Sidney area over recent years has been single-family, two- and three-bedroom homes. Some subdivisions have sidewalks, some don't. Streetlighting is sparse or nonexistent. There has been some apartment and condo-

"We like the peaceful setting of Sidney. It's such a relief from the noise of Calgary. Just what we pictured our retirement would be - only better."

- Retired Calgary oil executive

minium development but like Saanich, Sidney is more family-oriented. It has little appeal to singles because of its distance from downtown Victoria.

Home prices in Sidney have traditionally been five to 10 per cent below prices elsewhere in Greater Victoria. Distance from Victoria and lack of such municipal services as sidewalks, streetlighting and sewers account for much of that price difference. The location of a home relative to airport runways will also have its influence. Most homes have been built over the last 30 years.

Prior to its post-war growth, Sidney was a heavily-wooded area. To the credit of the various development companies, much of the timber has been retained in the residential areas, making it a very pleasant place to live.

Shopping is a comfortable exercise in Sidney.

Sidney

There are sufficient small stores scattered through the residential areas to meet immediate needs and the village offers most services along the main street, Beacon Avenue. Most things are available within walking distance. The village is adequately-stocked with banks, lawyers, doctors and dentists. There is a major food chain but no large department store.

There are two small recreation centres nearby and the Summergate Activities Council has a very active seniors activity centre which is something of a gathering place.

Besides its own weekly newspaper, The Sidney Review, the Victoria and Vancouver newspapers are also available for home delivery.

Esquimalt

Esquimalt is a separate municipality to the west of Victoria, governed by its own mayor and council and served by its own police and fire departments.

The municipality grew up around the Work Point army garrison, the Navy Base HMCS Naden and a federal government graving dock where ships hulls are cleaned.

Esquimalt is a mix of residential communities and commercial development with limited industry. It is populated primarily by armed forces families and civilian employees of the forces. Most of the retired people who live there are long-time residents. It is not an area that has catered to its retired population, nor has it made any great effort to attract retired people to reside there.

It is family-oriented, with children and pets in abundance. It is a pleasant community but not the choice for most in their retirement years.

Home prices in Esquimalt are on a par with James Bay. Its one exclusive residential area is located on the waterfront overlooking Victoria and Esquimalt harbors. In this wooded area, homes have an average price of about $100,000. It has a great number of apartment blocks where rents run from $300 to $500 a month.

Well-served by a great number of small corner stores, Esquimalt has a large shopping centre at its geographic centre, providing virtually any type of retail outlet or service required.

The weekly newspaper that serves this community is the Esquimalt Star. To subscribe, write 1620A Government Street, Victoria, V8W 1Z3.

Golfing in Victoria, Mount Baker in the background

Gulf Islands

L ocated in the Strait of Georgia between the southern end of Vancouver Island and the Lower Mainland is a group of small islands known as the Gulf Islands.

There are about 16 islands in the group, but only six of them have any sizable population. These islands include Saltspring, the largest, North and South Pender islands, Galiano, Mayne and Saturna. There are about 7,000 permanent residents of the six islands. Thirty per cent of them are at least 55 years old.

The islands have had a tremendous appeal because of the almost Mediterranean climate and the privacy afforded by living on a small island. Transportation to the islands from the mainland or Vancouver Island has, only in recent years, become relatively simple.

Residents are dependent on the B.C. Ferry system, private boats or aircraft to come and go from the islands. In the past, there have been proposals to build a bridge that would link the Lower Mainland to Vancouver Island via the Gulf Islands, but these are met with loud opposition from island residents eager to protect their private paradise. Fortunately for them, the chances of a bridge being built are, so far, quite remote.

It's the physical beauty that attracts most to the Gulf Islands. Like a siren to mariners, they can be too seductive, luring people to move without considering carefully the semi-isolation of small island life. There are some inconveniences to remote living. Your social life will be altered drastically by the scarcity of social amenities. Health services are more basic than in a city.

A couple of items are worth noting. Trespassing is a no-no. Islanders guard their privacy with great zeal. The beaches below the high water mark are for

"We really like it here, but we also know people who aren't so happy. We get to meet a lot of interesting people through our business, but we have friends who are widowers and they're quite lonely."

- Pender Island
hobby farmer

"I think the word you'd use to describe the people here is 'eclectic'."

everyone. Above the high water mark, you're trampling on someone's private turf.

And then there are dogs. Dogs running loose are viewed by most islanders as a threat, but especially by the many sheep farmers. They've had some nasty experiences in the past with household dogs running in packs to kill sheep. A leash is a must if you want your dog to live a long life.

Medical Services for Long-

In the adventure of planning a move to a new province, no one wants to assume that someday you may need long-term constant medical attention for such things as heart conditions, terminal illnesses, or multiple sclerosis.

Still, it will be worthwhile knowing how you might be taken care of in British Columbia if it comes to that.

Residential care is intended for those who cannot adequately care for themselves, or cannot be cared for at home. If you live in an urban centre, you would most likely be placed in one through the long term care department of a hospital. In smaller communities, you would contact a local health unit.

Placement can take a considerable length of time in some communities. If your situation is urgent, it may be possible to speed up the process. If possible, you should make a personal visit to several facilities before deciding to move.

Care facilities are operated by non-profit associations or private owners, but are licensed and regulated by the Provincial Adult Care Facilities Licensing Board. Operators are obligated to provide safe and proper care. To obtain a list of various facilities, contact the continuing care di-

"We're actually bored, if you want the truth. If we could afford it, we'd prefer to live in Vancouver or Victoria to be close to better medical centres. It makes us both nervous to be way out here by ourselves, but we just can't afford to move anywhere else. We're also kind of lonely, but there isn't too much to do out here."

- Pender Island couple

Weather

Lying in a sheltered zone between the east coast of Vancouver Island and the Mainland, the islands enjoy the mildest weather in Canada. They have the longest frost-free season in the country - eight months.

The average temperature is 10 degrees Celsius. The average ranges seasonally between 2 Celsius and 23 Celsius. Average rainfall is about 54 cm, well below Victoria and Vancouver rainfalls. The islands

"Yes. It rains, but I've always associated islands with water, so it doesn't bother me."

Term Medical Needs

vision of the Ministry of Health in Victoria at 1515 Blanshard Street, V8W 3C8.

Short stay and 'assessment and treatment' centres are used for older people whose diagnosis is difficult and treatment is complex. These centres are located at Vancouver General Hospital, St. Joseph's Hospital in Vancouver and Royal Jubilee Hospital in Victoria. Referrals must be made by your family doctor.

Hospice programs are designed to provide compassionate care to terminally-ill individuals and their families. This care may be provided at home, in the hospice unit of a hospital or a combination of the two. Most major hospitals that provide this care rely on professionals and trained volunteers.

Family hospitals offer rehabilitation programs for such conditions as strokes, multiple sclerosis, fractures, amputations, and arthritis. They use a volunteer-team approach, and the family is actively involved.

Group homes are privately run, housing five to eight residents. Charges for this type of accommodation are more expensive than government homes. Residential care in public homes costs $15.50 per day and private care homes are about $20.

"We have always wanted to live this sort of life and are very grateful that we can afford it, financially, since we found land prices extremely expensive.

- Saltspring Island resident

also escape much of the wind that hits coastal communities. Summers are dry and cool, winters, damp and mild.

Housing

Trying to come up with an average home or property price is difficult.

Property values tend to fluctuate. After World War II, many B.C. residents moved to the islands to operate small farms. They were followed by people who wanted summer homes. With this rise in demand, property values rose. But as property changes hands now, prices fluctuate with the financial circumstances of the vendor.

The cost of goods and services are on a par with the rest of southwestern British Columbia, although food tends to be a bit higher

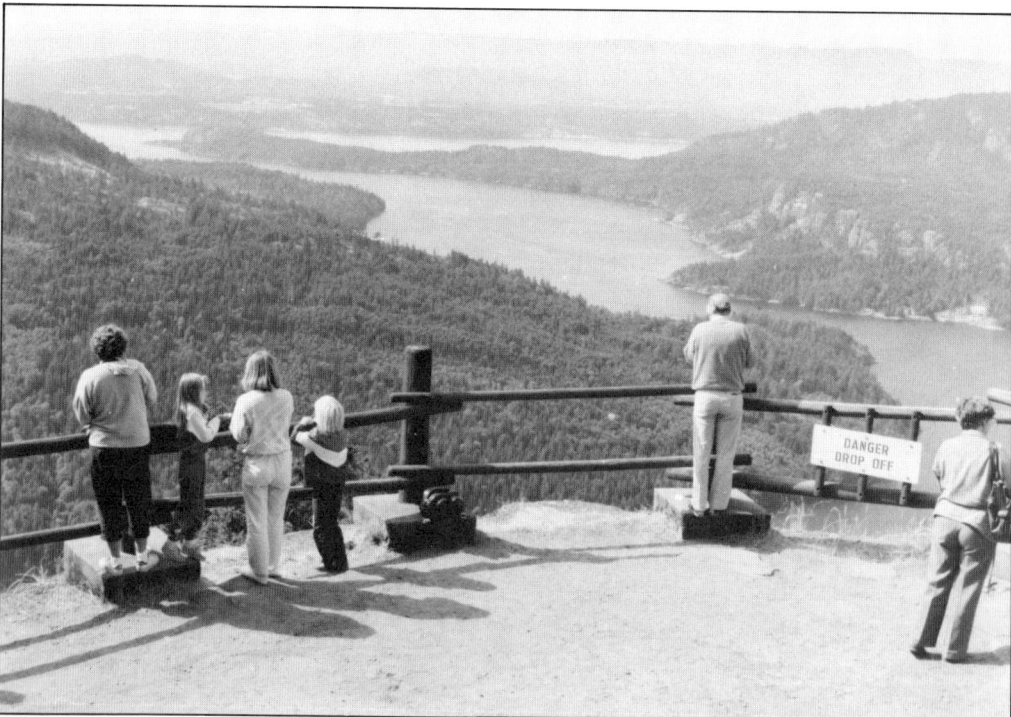

Medical Services

The only acute care hospital in the Gulf Islands is Lady Minto Hospital at Ganges on Saltspring Island. Potential retirees to the Gulf Islands should carefully consider their present and future medical needs prior to making a decision on which Gulf Island they might wish to settle. While all of the islands have some medical care available, a retiree with, for example, a heart condition might wish to consider a locale where emergency health services can provide extremely rapid response in the case of a heart attack or other such emergency.

In addition, the islands offer virtually no specialist medical services. Residents requiring the services of, for example, an ophthamologist or internal medicine specialist, would have to travel to Victoria to see a doctor there. And that will consume most of any day, when one considers the necessity of a ferry trip.

Shopping and Transportation

There's little 'running to the corner store' on the islands. There aren't that many of them.

Shopping is restricted to one village and usually one store on each island. On Saltspring, that's Ganges, though there are small communities at Fulford Harbor, Fernwood and Vesuvius Bay. On Galiano Island, it's Sturdies Bay. Mayne Island has Miners Bay and Village Bay. On Saturna Island, it's Saturna and on North Pender Island, there are Port Washington and Hope Bay.

As would be expected, they carry essentials. Major shopping has to be done either in Vancouver, Victoria, Crofton or Nanaimo. Mail order shopping is a way of life but that usually involves some added delivery costs.

"I don't think this would be a very good place for someone with health problems to retire, it's just too isolated."

- Galiano resident

"If a couple had a very limited budget, I don't think that any area on the Gulf Islands would be suitable for retirement because you couldn't be close to any necessary social services. You need a vehicle."

- Saltspring Island resident

There is no public transportation system here. Islanders get around their particular island generally by car, but also by bicycle, motorcycles, boats and even walking.

Getting off the island is another matter. Ferries service the main islands from both the mainland and Vancouver Island. Reservations are accepted for passage between Tsawwassen and the Gulf Islands, but not between Swartz Bay and the islands or between individual islands. Reservations are not required for foot passengers, since they are always boarded. Sailings are frequent each day, but heavy tourist traffic in summer can mean two- and three-hour waits.

Residents use their private boats to get around their islands and while there is no regular air service, chartered aircraft operate on the islands.

Recreation, Entertainment, News, Radio and TV

"We just want to enjoy each other's company by ourselves, we had six children and have never had much time to ourselves. So we just enjoy being alone, sailing wherever we feel like."

- Pender Island couple

There is limited organized recreation and entertainment on the Gulf Islands and for the most part, in rugged individualist style, islanders seek out their own forms of relaxation and activity. Individual sports like horseback riding and fishing are popular, and this is a superlative setting in which to do both. Marinas at Ganges on Saltspring, Montague Harbor on Galiano and Otter Bay on North Pender Island, serve the fishing community.

Recreation is a local activity. Most island communities have some sort of recreation centre and there is a provincial park on all of the main islands.

There are a few organizations such as the Golden Agers Centre at Ganges, an activity centre for senior citizens. The Galiano Community Hall on Sturdies Bay Road offers programs for all ages and social and recreational programs designed especially to appeal to seniors.

The Gulf Islands Community Arts Council is prominent in organizing activities centred around the growing cottage crafts industry on the islands.

Clubs and groups on the islands include a local rod and gun club on Saltspring, a Masonic lodge and three golf clubs, one each on Galiano, Pender and Saltspring islands. Galiano's and Pender's are public courses. Saltspring's is private. Green fees range among the three from $5 to $12.

There are a few restaurants on the island, but no commercial night life. There isn't even a theatre.

"If you're going to live on the Gulf Islands, you need to be reasonably active and healthy, and have an intense hobby. Otherwise, you're going to be unhappy and extremely bored, especially if you're without any family."

- Pender Island
hobby farmer

"We wanted a setting that is typically 'west coast' but couldn't afford the sites we liked on the mainland."

- Saltspring Island resident

Parksville-Qualicum

This long-time summer recreation area, popular with Vancouver Islanders for its long, wide, hard sand beaches and its salmon fishing, has in more recent years become a favorite retirement area.

The two communities, only a couple of miles apart, have over the years merged into one beachfront development extending for several miles. The total population of the two villages is less than 10,000.

Included in this combined area, just over 160 kilometres north of Victoria on the Island Highway, are the even smaller communities of Errington, Coombs and Hilliers. At one time, Hilliers housed a large Doukhobor population. But all that remains is a few buildings left standing after the Doukhobors moved east into the Kootenay Valley.

There is little industry in the area. The major money maker for both communities is the summertime visitor industry and a brisk convention business the year round. It is a favorite salmon fishing area. There are few days any season of the year when there aren't several small boats trolling off the beaches.

Scenery, the long beaches, shallow warm water and mild climate are the major attractions of the Parksville-Qualicum area. It is a typical summer community, busy from May to September with thousands of tourists. It is a quiet, pleasant and friendly area to be year-round.

Parksville-Qualicum has become popular because it is small, well-serviced and close enough to larger cities that it is not isolated from the amenities of the metropolitan areas.

Like White Rock, you have to accept the company

Playing ball near Parksville's sandy beach

"Actually, we used to have a house that was closer to Parksville but we moved after a year or two because we just found it too busy. We much prefer Qualicum."

of summer beach crowds if you want to retire here. They come with the territory. It is certainly a friendly area, and it is also a major location for the Vancouver Island arts community.

Weather

Located on Vancouver Island's east coast, Parksville-Qualicum boasts short, mild winters and warm, dry summers with enough rain to keep it green, but far less than the mainland coastal areas that lie just across the Strait of Georgia.

Annual temperatures range from one or two Celsius during the coldest part of the winter to the low 20s in the spring, summer and fall.

Housing

Finding a moderately-priced home is a simple matter.

During the heady days of the early 1980's, when new homes were selling faster than they could be built, subdivision and home building boomed. When the bubble finally burst, many developers were left holding a large inventory of building lots and completed houses. This resulted in a buyers' market that still exists.

The average selling price of a home is about $60,000 with new two- and three-bedroom ranchers (no basement) averaging $50,000. Ocean front and view properties sell for slightly more.

There are some condominiums selling for about the same price as private homes. The few apartments there are rent for between $300 and $500 a month. There are no housing cooperatives.

Recognizing the area as a choice retirement site, there are a number of housing developments located a few miles south of Parksville-Qualicum at French Creek, built with retired tenants in mind. One of the largest, Eaglecrest, borders an 18-hole

"Well, we live off the beaten track in Parksville, so we don't notice the crowds and if we do want to go to the beach, we know a few around here that aren't as crowded. Plus we ski and golf during the winter, so we have lots to do around here."

golf course where you can play year-round. There are also a number of mobile home parks that provide low-cost, low-maintenance accommodation and cater to the retirement community. Further information about real estate in the area can be obtained from the Vancouver Island Real Estate Board, Box 719, Nanaimo, B.C., V9B 5M2.

Medical Services

There are more than 20 doctors in the Parksville-Qualicum region and substantially more when Nan-

"We'd rather go somewhere else, like Qualicum, for the summer because of all the tourists."

Traffic line up in Parksville, a common summer site at its main intersection

aimo and the Comox-Courtenay areas, both less than an hour away, are taken into consideration.

There are numerous clinics in the area and provincial ambulance service is available. The nearest hospital is the Nanaimo Regional General Hospital, less than an hour's drive south.

At Qualicum, land has already been set aside for a local hospital but, so far, there has been no financial support offered by the province. A major campaign is underway by local residents for a medical facility.

There are three long-term care facilities in the area: Trillium Lodge, with 50 beds; Arrowsmith Lodge, 58 beds and Arranglen Lodge, with 86 beds. Funding has been approved for a 150-bed extended care unit at Nanaimo Regional General Hospital.

Recreation, Entertainment, News, Radio and TV

There is one seniors activity centre in the immediate area, the Seniors Drop-In Centre in Parksville. There is also a seniors centre at Nanaimo, and another at Comox.

Most major service clubs are represented on one or the other of the villages and there are two golf courses, both public, both nine holes and both at Qualicum.

At Qualicum, there is a movie theatre and a very active theatre company with its own 180-seat theatre which is also used by touring performers.

Qualicum offers excellent lawn bowling greens and Parksville will soon be adding them at its popular community park on Parksville Bay.

And then, there's fishing. Fishermen have the best of both worlds in this area. As well as excellent salmon fishing right off shore, there is an abundance of fresh water fishing at nearby Englishman River, Little Qualicum River and Big Qualicum River. They

"Well, to meet people, I go to the community rec centre. It may not be much by your standards, but we like it."

are all well-known on Vancouver Island for their steelhead salmon fishing.

The local weekly newspapers are the Parksville-Qualicum News and the Arrowsmith Star. Their addresses are Box 1300 (The Star) and Box 2579 (The News), Parksville, B.C. V0R 2S0. Vancouver and Victoria dailies are available.

Shopping and Transportation

Shopping for daily necessities is as convenient as it can get. As well as a substantial number of small corner-type convenience stores, there is a large shopping mall located between Parksville and Qualicum.

There is a major grocery outlet surrounded by many small specialty shops in Qualicum's well-planned central core. A liquor store and post office are all within easy walking distance.

Parksville has two large grocery outlets and a wide variety of specialty shops. Both communities have several banks and credit unions. The area is probably not the best place to make major purchases, like a fridge or color television. But the trip to Nanaimo, 45 kilometres to the south, will net you the best selection and deals in the area

The only local transit service is taxi. But the Island Highway offers excellent access to Nanaimo to the south and Comox-Courtenay to the north.

B.C. Ferry service to the Mainland is about 30 minutes away by car at Departure Bay. Vancouver Island Coachlines and Via Rail offer daily service south to Victoria.

Two regional air carriers offer service to Vancouver International Airport. Pacific Western Airlines offers a regularly-scheduled service out of Comox, about an hour's drive north of Qualicum. Cassidy Airport, south of Nanaimo, also services Vancouver with a choice of flights.

"I suppose it's the people here that make it all worth-while. We probably couldn't manage on our own still if we didn't have such helpful neighbors."

Beach promenade at Qualicum

Beach near Comox airbase

Comox Valley

Vancouver Island's storm-ravaged west coast has earned an international marine reputation as being one of the most dangerous areas of the world in which to sail.

But little more than 80 kilometres away, the sheltered east coast boasts warm, shallow waters, long wide sand beaches, far less wind and a temperate climate.

The Comox Valley, about 300 kilometres north of Victoria and about 70 kilometres north of Parksville, is one of the favored Island areas for both retirement and vacationing. Although there is easy access to both Vancouver and Victoria, both are at least three hours away.

The two largest cities in the Comox Valley are Courtenay with a population of about 10,000 and Comox, about five kilometres away on a small peninsula with a population of some 7,000. Together with the surrounding areas, the total population is about 40,000. Over the past number of years, the average annual growth rate in population has been about 2.4 per cent.

The valley has a large retired population - about 16 per cent over 60 years old - with plenty of activities designed to accommodate seniors.

The Comox Valley has all the scenic beauty imaginable; mountains, forests and miles of beaches. Small farms make it a photographer's and painter's paradise. And for those contemplating the practical aspects of retirement, the picture is even brighter.

There is little industry here. Small farms and tourism, connected largely with the winter sports on Mount Washington and Forbidden Plateau, provide most people their living. Comox is a Canadian Forces

Base and, as well as providing the largest single source of employment, the base also provides a familiar drone from jet engines. For those who like airshows, this is a bonus because the Snowbirds, Canada's aerobatic team, often come there to practice.

Forestry employs about 1,300 people in the Courtenay/Comox area and still figures prominently in the economy despite the recent slump in the industry. There are also large silviculture nurseries in the valley.

About three-quarters of the land in the Comox Valley is held in small acreages within the Agricultural Land Reserve. Those small holdings are often dairy and vegetable farms.

Courtenay from the air

Weather

"The weather? I could do without the clouds in the wintertime, but it sure rains a lot less here than on the mainland."

The valley enjoys a moderate, Pacific coast climate, characterized by short, mild winters and warm, dry summers. It receives its fair share of rain during the winter months, but escapes the seasonal storms of the west and southern coasts. Annual rainfall averages about 1200 mm to 1400 mm.

Annual temperatures range from one or two Celsius in the coldest winter months to the high 20s through late spring and summer. Daily mean temperatures average 2 degrees Celsius in January and 17 degrees in July. Moving away from the sea towards the mountains, winters are a little crisper and summers a little hotter.

A recent Comox Valley Chamber of Commerce survey of retired people showed that the climate was the major reason for their choice of the area.

Housing

The average selling price of a single-family home is about $60,000, well below the price paid for similar accommodation in Vancouver or Victoria. Of course, size and choice location can send prices soaring to $125,000 or $150,000.

Rental accommodation is on a par with most other communities, running $300 to $400 a month. There are no cooperative housing projects in the valley.

Three-quarters of the housing stock in the Comox Valley is comprised of single-family, detached dwellings. That's substantially higher than the B.C. average which is about 60 per cent. In recent years in the valley, duplexes and apartments have been increasing their share of the remaining 25 per cent of the housing stock.

"I live here because of the people. Really, I've had no difficulty making new friends since I moved here two years ago."

Medical Services

St. Joseph's General Hospital in Comox serves the entire valley with its 220 acute and extended care beds. It provides modern radiology and physiotherapy, outpatient services, diabetic daycare, dietetic counselling and a Meals on Wheels service for the housebound. It has 76 extended care beds.

Cumberland Diagnostic and Treatment Centre provides 50 intermediate care beds and there are six medical clinics staffed by 39 doctors.

Shopping and Transportation

Like most small communities that have begun to grow, both Comox and Courtenay offer a wide variety of shopping. There is no shortage of the small grocery and convenience stores in residential neighborhoods. There are two major shopping malls, the Driftwood and the Comox, providing a wide variety of goods and services.

The area also has several branches of all the major banks, four credit unions, a trust company and several investment and financial planning outlets.

Anything that cannot be supplied by the valley stores and malls can be found in the numerous large shopping malls of Nanaimo, about two hours drive south.

The valley is served for access to the outside world in several ways - highway, air, boat or rail.

Time Air and B.C. Air operate daily service between Comox and Vancouver. Via Rail's Esquimalt and Nanaimo Railway (the E & N) operates a daily connection between Courtenay and Victoria. Schedules are subject to seasonal change. Island Coach Lines offers regular bus service between the valley and all island points.

"I love gardening and I just love it here because I can grow such a variety of plants and flowers.

B.C. Ferries connects directly from the Comox Valley with the ferry to Powell River on the mainland. Departure Bay at Nanaimo is also within easy reach for connection to Vancouver.

Recreation, Entertainment, News, Radio and TV

There is one seniors activity centre in Comox, and two others in nearby communities a short drive away. D'Esterre House Senior Citizens Centre in Comox is a busy and popular gathering place for seniors, as is Evergreen Seniors operating out of the Sid Williams Civic Theatre in Courtenay. The latter group also operates the Courtenay Recreation As-

Downtown Courtenay

sociation with many of its programs designed for seniors.

The major service clubs are represented in the valley. Both cities have excellent libraries, reading rooms and bookmobile services.

There are two public golf courses, the 18-hole Sunnydale Golf Society course just north of Courtenay and Longlands Par-3 Golf Course near Comox. A third course, the nine-hole Comox Golf Club, is semi-private.

Near this area is one of the largest parks in the provincial system, Strathcona Provincial Park, with excellent fishing and hiking. There is no hunting inside the park and, in fact, if you're a first-time hunter, you must complete a hunter education course if you want to hunt anywhere in the province.

Skiing is also close at hand - Mount Washington for the downhill skiers and Forbidden Plateau for the cross-country skiers.

There are facilities here also for the curler, swimmer and lawn bowler.

The Comox Valley is in recent years becoming known as a centre for the arts, with an annual summer music festival, an active theatre group, an arts council and art galleries that exhibit the works of local artists and artisans. That means there are plenty of opportunities not only to buy artwork and crafts, but also to learn to do them.

"We like it here because I golf a lot and we can golf all year long here."

Filberg Lodge in Comox

Okanagan Lake at Kelowna

Okanagan Valley

British Columbia's popular Okanagan Valley lies about 450 kilometres east of Vancouver. It is a long, arid valley, oriented north-south and running for about 160 kilometres north from the American border.

In the centre of the valley is Okanagan Lake, about 120 kilometres long with the valley's three major cities on its shores: Penticton, at the south end of the lake; Kelowna, about midway up the lake; and Vernon, at its north end. Between Penticton and Kelowna are two smaller communities - Summerland and Peachland.

Since the turn of the century, Okanagan Valley has been the province's prime tree fruit farming area. Its apples, peaches and apricots were exported world wide. In recent years, production costs and other economic factors have brought hard times to the industry. Many farmers have ripped up their orchards, subdivided and sold their land for residential or commercial development to meet the growing demands of summer visitors.

Grape growers have found a new lease on life, however. Okanagan and Lower Mainland wineries, using Okanagan grown grapes, are producing world class wines and are flourishing. Grapes have filled the vacuum left by the sagging tree fruit industry.

The valley still has a successful fruit processing industry, producing canned fruit, fruit juice, jam and jelly and fruit candy. A can manufacturing plant finds clients right in the valley.

A number of small industries have moved into the valley, notably manufacturers of mobile homes, trailers, trucks, and recreation vehicles. There is also a sawmill and planer mill industry but it too is suffering from an economic downturn. Retirement communities and tourism have become two rapidly growing industries throughout the length of the valley.

Outdoor recreation is a major activity for valley people. The warm weather and warm waters of Okanagan Lake and smaller adjoining lakes spawn every kind of water-oriented activity in the late spring and summer. In winter, the whole valley offers a variety of winter sport opportunities, patronized heavily by both local residents and visitors.

Weather

"Actually, we retired with friends and they had family in the Okanagan, so here we are. The weather here is lovely. No bugs in the summer was one plus and not so cold in the winter. That was another plus."

- Retired motel owner from Meadow Lake, Sask.

Because of the valley's interior location, weather extremes are more noticeable here than on the coast. Summers are warm and dry. Winters are colder than the coast, but very liveable and normally with less snow than the rest of the province or the prairie provinces.

The first snow usually arrives sometime in December and the last snowfall normally occurs in late February. Mean maximum temperatures for January are about 0 degree Celsius while mean July maximums are about 28 degrees Celsius.

Touring a winery in Kelowna

It is a dry climate and the area is not subject to the severe winter and spring storms that lash the coastal communities. It also has much less rain than the coast. On these counts, the Okanagan is credited with some benefit to those suffering from arthritis and respiratory ailments such as asthma. The sun shines an average of 2,000 hours each year and there is always a light breeze.

Weather conditions throughout the valley are more uniform than on the coast. When it is sunny, it is sunny everywhere. Looking at the three major cities of the valley as potential retirement sites, there is little difference between them with regard to weather.

Transportation

Commuting between Vernon, Kelowna, Penticton and the smaller communities on the lakeshore is relatively simple. It is not uncommon for people to work in one city and live in another. The highway is always busy but well-maintained both winter and summer. Highway construction now underway or planned will see improvements between the Okanagan cities and a major new connector to the Lower Mainland - the Coquihalla Highway, to be completed sometime in the future. At this writing, the Coquihalla Highway was finished between Merritt and Hope, with further plans to connect it with the Okanagan. The existing connections to the Lower Mainland include Highway No. 3 near the American border via Princeton and Hope, and Highway No. 1 via the Fraser Canyon.

The largest airport in the valley is just north of Kelowna providing frequent air service east and west with Pacific Western Airlines, Air BC, CP Air and Time Air. During the winter months, air travel is sometimes interrupted by fog. Vernon, only 40 kilometres to the north, is also served by the Kelowna airport. Vernon's municipal airport is restricted to small aircraft. Penticton, 55 kilometres south of Kelowna, has its own airport, served by Pacific Western Airlines.

Kelowna, Vernon and Penticton each have their own city transit systems. Bus schedules vary in frequency according to the time of day and amount of traffic. Just how much you will need a vehicle depends on the community. In Vernon, for example, a car is not essential for downtown shopping, though it is certainly a convenience. Penticton, on the other hand, is more spread out than Vernon and a car would be more a necessity than a convenience.

Weather and transportation are aspects of valley life that can be addressed easily together for all three communities. Now we'll look at the more local aspects of housing, medical services, shopping, recreation and entertainment for each community.

Kelowna

Kelowna is the largest of the three Okanagan cities with a total population, including nearby Westbank and Peachland, of 97,000. People over the age of 55 comprise about 26 per cent of that total. Kelowna is becoming more and more a retirement centre, primarily because its younger population is moving away to distant employment opportunities.

Because of its climate and its rural atmosphere, it is a pleasant, friendly place to live. Average annual precipitation is 33 cm. It is normally frost free from May to October.

Housing

The average price of housing in the Okanagan does not mean all that much. Real estate in and around Kelowna can vary from very old and small to very new on substantial acreage. Prices can be extremely high. Waterfront properties and benchland sites overlooking the lake are also expensive.

Within the city, small two and three-bedroom

"We love the weather here. The winters are so mild and the summers are very pleasant. They'd be unbearable without the breeze. Kelowna is a nice size for us. It is not big, but it still has all the amenities we need."

- Retired implement dealer from Red Deer

homes are in the $50,000 to $60,000 range, but that describes a narrow range of the market outside of which prices vary widely. Even outside of the city, where there are no municipal services, acreage, view lots and houses are hundreds of thousands of dollars, largely because many choice properties are being held as investments rather than as residences.

There are several seniors housing developments in and around Kelowna. Most have been built by either a service club or a church. Costs, availability, services and eligibility requirements vary. Most have waiting lists. The best source of information about these developments is through one of the many senior citizen activity centres or the Kelowna Chamber of Commerce, 544 Harvey Street, Kelowna, V7Y 7N8

There are three housing cooperatives in the Kelowna area, but like cooperatives elsewhere in B.C.,

"It's certainly been a tough adjustment for us because we left behind some life-long friends and, of course, family. We like Kelowna. We love the weather and the people seem friendly, but it isn't the same as Camrose with old friends."

- Farmer from Camrose

Monsters to choose from

No place seems to be complete without at least one unexplained monster. B.C. has three.

The oldest is Okanagan Lake's Ogopogo, a serpent-like creature that is seen from time to time but has never been authenticated. Lots of photographs have surfaced but they have proven to be less than conclusive.

Victoria's monster is known as Cadborosaurus, nicknamed 'Caddy', after a local bay. Again, photographs but nothing authenticated.

Then there's the Sasquatch, claimed to reside in the area of Aggasiz in the Fraser Valley. This apparently-apelike creature is described by those who claim to have seen it as standing seven feet tall, covered with hair and having a horrendous body stench. Again no authentication.

Of course, in some ways, it is good that these creatures have not been captured. Life would be rather dull if there wasn't some unexplained mystery to puzzle over. British Columbians are luckier than most.

there is a waiting list. There is no central cooperative office. Application must be made to individual cooperatives. The addresses are: Okanagan Housing Cooperative, Box 2352, Station R, Kelowna, B.C. V1X 6A5; Southgate Housing Cooperative, 116, 1961 Dunn Street, Kelowna, B.C. V1Y 4C4; and Central Okanagan Housing Cooperative, Box 909, Westbank, B.C. V0H 2A0.

Kelowna has no municipally-operated garbage collection service. Private pick-up service is about $6 a month. Annual property taxes average between $900 and $1,100 a year, less the provincial home owner grant of $380 ($630 for those over 65 years of age).

Medical Service

Kelowna General Hospital is also a regional hospital, serving the whole Okanagan Valley with 563 beds, 250 of which are for extended care. It also has a large emergency ward and is served by the B.C. Ambulance Association.

In addition, there is an 80-bed intermediate care facility, Three Links Manor, and some 14 facilities that fall into the categories of nursing home or rest home for the elderly.

Kelowna is home to about 135 doctors and 48 dentists.

Shopping

The largest shopping centre in the valley in fact, the largest mall between Calgary and Vancouver, locals claim - is the Orchard Park Regional Shopping Centre located about five kilometres from the centre of the city. The centre is served by the municipal bus service and houses Hudson's Bay, Sears and Woolco plus a wide variety of other retail and service outlets.

Kelowna has several shopping malls, large and small, a core commercial district of retail outlets and scattered grocery stores, often only a couple of blocks walking distance from home.

"I suppose that big shopping mall is the best place to go because you can get it all done at once. But it is tiring, you know."

- About Orchard Park in Kelowna

Recreation, Entertainment, News, Radio and TV

As a major destination for summer recreation, Kelowna's recreational amenities focus on the lake and water sports in general - swimming, fishing, and sailing. For example, there are three yacht clubs and five marinas in the immediate area. And there are numerous beach developments on Okanagan Lake and nearby Wood and Kalamalka lakes.

But recreational opportunities are by no means second rate in other sports. There are four 18-hole golf courses in the immediate area, three of them public, with green fees running from $13 to $25. In addition to those, there are a handful of nine-hole courses, a par-3 and a couple of driving ranges.

Tennis courts are scattered throughout the city and there are three curling clubs, four skating rinks, two indoor swimming pools, five bowling alleys and a lawn bowling club. Recreation centres and the YM-YWCA offer some special programs for seniors.

If skiing in your retirement strikes your fancy, there are four ski resorts within two hours of Kelowna - Big White, Last Mountain, Apex Alpine and Silver Star.

Kelowna's community theatre seats about 900 for concerts and plays. Two theatre companies are active, the Kelowna Theatre Society and the Sunshine Theatre Society.

For the celluloid variety of theatre, Orchard Park has two cinemas and there are four others, one of which is a drive-in theatre. Kelowna is also home to six art galleries and the Kelowna Centennial Museum and National Exhibition Centre.

Kelowna is the home of a mid-summer regatta. There are a host of other activities besides the racing of boats but in recent years, the festivities have been marred by public drunkenness and vandalism, nearly to the point of rioting.

"When you can get in, The Kelowna Golf and Country Club has a real good course."

- Retired Kelowna golfer

"Well, that retired seniors citizens Centre is probably the best around here. The seniors themselves get involved in volunteering and what-not. They've got just about anything you'd want to do."

- Kelowna senior citizen

Seniors activity centres abound in and around Kelowna, all offering a wide variety of services and recreational activities. A typical roster of activities for the Retired Citizens' Activity Centre, for example, would include duplicate bridge, bowling, dances, stageband concerts and floor curling.

There are six radio stations in the area: CKOV, CKIQ, CHIM-FM, SILK-FM, CBC-FM and CBC French service; one local TV station, CHBC and on cable, a wide variety of Canadian and American channels. There is also pay TV, at an extra cost. Initial hook up at this writing was $21.60 with a monthly rental fee of $10.26. Fee for pay channels was $21.90 per month.

There is one daily newspaper, The Kelowna Courier, and the weekly Kelowna Capitol News. Vancouver dailies are also available by subscription. To subscribe to the Courier, write 550 Doyle Avenue, Kelowna, V1Y 7V1, Telephone (604) 762-4445.

"For coffee, I go to the retirement centre downtown. The coffee isn't all that outstanding but the company is."

- Retired Kelowna resident

"We stay here because of the weather, not the people. It's a nice city in all the things it has to offer but the people aren't too friendly."

- Retired farmer
from Stettler, Alberta

Sailing on Okanagan Lake

Vernon

Vernon is located about 55 kilometres north of Kelowna at the north end of Okanagan Lake, and is the second largest city in the valley. About 39,000 people live here at the centre of logging and ranching in the valley.

With weather conditions the same as the rest of the valley, Vernon can be a very nice community to live in. Because of its size, it does not offer all of the services available in Kelowna.

Each January, Vernon is the site of one of the best winter carnivals in the valley. Nearby Kalamalka and Long Lake regions are popular camping and holidaying areas during the summer months.

Like Kelowna and Penticton, the cost of living is a little higher than the Lower Mainland. But if a quiet retirement city is being sought, Vernon fits the bill.

Housing

Private home prices in Vernon are comparable to those of Kelowna, averaging about $63,000 for a single-family, two- or three-bedroom house. Municipal taxes are slightly higher than Kelowna, at about $1,125. New homes are going up on the outskirts of the city and the waterfront attracts a mix of large, expensive homes, many of them costing more than $100,000, and small cottages, also prized for their location.

There are a few other housing options which are well-used in Vernon, moreso than in the other Okanagan communities - apartments and mobile homes. There is a good stock of apartments and several townhouse rental complexes. Average monthly rental is in the $500 range.

A local real estate firm, Bertram and Co. Realty Ltd. publishes a real estate directory for Vernon, listing and describing what is for sale. The firm's address is 3100 32nd Avenue, Vernon, B.C. V1T 2L9.

"We couldn't put up with the dampness in Comox, so we did some checking around and discovered that the interior was dryer than the coast. We also learned that most of the retirees in the Okanagan come from Alberta. That certainly is true in Vernon."

- Retired businessman
from Grand Prairie

"It's always windy here. It drives me crazy."

- Vernon

"I wish it wasn't so cold in the winter. Going outside to run errands becomes such a chore."

- Vernon

Blue Skies Housing Cooperative, at 4420 Bella Vista Road, offers a compromise between outright purchase and simply renting. This development is in the style of townhouses.

Shopping

Vernon's central commercial area is the life of the retail scene in the city, with the only Eaton's department store in the valley, Woolco, Zeller's and a variety of smaller retail outlets and grocery stories.

There are two mall developments, the Village Green and Polson Place malls.

Medical Services

Vernon's Jubilee Hospital has 343 beds, about 225 of them for acute care, and an emergency ward. There is an extended care unit adjoining the hospital with 188 beds. The city is also served by the regional hospital at Kelowna.

Vernon has no shortage of doctors or dentists. Homes for the elderly and nursing homes are also in good supply here, though costs vary with the service offered. Further information on these homes can be obtained from the Vernon Chamber of Commerce, 3700 33rd Street, Vernon, V1T 5T6.

Recreation, Entertainment, News, Radio and TV

Vernon is the closest of the three Okanagan cities to Silver Star Ski Area. The resort is only 22 kilometres away, and has seven lifts and about 35 different runs, from novice or expert in degree of difficulty.

Vernon Golf and Country Club and Spallumcheen Golf and Tennis Club both have 18-hole courses, the latter, as the name implies, with tennis courts.

The local parks and recreation department operates a complete array of recreational facilities, including a skating arena, an outdoor rink, a curling rink, a swimming pool, tennis courts and a lawn bowling green.

In Vernon, good things come in threes, it seems, with three art galleries, three museums, three cinemas and three public libraries. One of those museums is the widely-known O'Keefe Historical Ranch, a re-creation of a pioneer ranch. Powerhouse Theatre is the local theatre group.

Three seniors activity centres in or near Vernon offer a full range of recreational activities. A recreation centre in the city has a wide range of physical fitness programs for seniors. And Vernon has an interesting 'volunteer grandparents' program for seniors who would like surrogate grandchildren closeby.

The Vernon Daily News is the only local daily newspaper, located at 3309 31st Avenue, Vernon, V1T 1Z2, Telephone (604) 545-0671. The Lower Mainland dailies are available by subscription. There are two local radio stations, CKAL and CJIB, but no local television station. Cable and pay television services are the same as Kelowna.

"There are probably two nursing homes that stand out as being better than the rest. One of them is the long term centre that's beside the Schubert Centre. Also, I know there's a long waiting list for that highrise complex behind Eatons, the Bethany home. I suppose they're so popular because they're right downtown. It's not so far for shopping and for those who are active enough, they can go to the Schubert Centre."

- Vernon

Penticton

Penticton is the smallest of the three major valley centres, with a population of 30,500. But it is also the most popular with summer visitors.

The city has two warm lakes to choose from - Okanagan Lake on the north boundary and the smaller but popular Skaha Lake at the south. During the summer months, Penticton is packed with tourists, most of them campers. Winter is a quiet time.

Of the three valley cities, Penticton is the one which has progressed the fastest, propelled mostly by tourism. What it lost in the decline of the tree fruit industry, it has made up in tourist attractions.

Living costs are comparable to other Okanagan

"I suppose that as far as rest homes go, this one is okay. Guess my daughter-in-law got tired of putting up with me. They hardly ever come to visit me, you know. But the people here are friendly and I never lack for company. The people from that place next door (Schubert) come over quite often and we sometimes play cards."

- Vernon widow

"We left Kelowna because it was just too big for us. I guess we're just small town people. Penticton is more interesting than other places we've been in, plus it's friendly."

communities, and it has good transportation service in and out by bus and air service.

There is some light industry, but not enough to take away from its weather and scenic attractions. Its weather conditions parallel those of Kelowna and Vernon, though it claims to be a bit milder in winter and warmer in summer. Locals may not so eagerly point to persistent breezes in the area.

Housing

The average home price is $66,000. Annual property taxes average about $1,400, the highest in the valley. Average monthly rents are in the $550 range, though there are few apartment blocks here in comparison with Vernon. Single family, detached dwellings are the norm.

Common cents

If you are considering a major relocation, you should review the overall structuring of your financial affairs.

If you are going to liquidate your assets when you retire and resettle, there may be adjustments that can be made to ease the tax bite.

Consider placing all assets in joint tenancy so that, on the death of one spouse, the survivor can take title without the need to probate the will.

If you have liquidated your assets, this may not be the time of your life when you want to fret over each investment decision. Should you consider enlisting some professional management expertise? In the last few years, major trust companies have developed a market in so-called 'agency accounts.' Individuals place their investments with the trust company for administration. The arrangements are very flexible, ranging from 'custodianship' where the trust company simply acts as an umbrella and provides a record keeping service to 'discretionary'

Penticton was a major fruit growing area years ago. Today, many of its orchards have been replaced by residential and commercial development, mostly motels and hotels. Some fruit is still grown.

There is only one cooperative housing development in Penticton, Clarendon Hall Housing Cooperative, 111 - 115 Warren Avenue West, Penticton, V2A 7N5. Application must be made to the cooperative itself. There is a waiting list and you must be at least 55 years of age to apply.

Medical Services

Penticton has its own general hospital with 264 beds, 63 of which are reserved for extended care. It is also served by the Kelowna regional hospital.

agencies where the trust company makes investment decisions for you after working out an overall investment strategy with you. The fees for these agency services are generally tax deductible.

Finally, have you considered what might happen if you or your spouse become mentally incompetent? Although informal arrangements can be put into place to administer the affairs of an incompetent spouse, quite often the only course of action is to apply for a Committee Order in the Supreme Court, which is both expensive and time-consuming. If is far better to consider the use of the Continuing General Power of Attorney which can provide full management authority over a person's affairs in the event of a subsequent affliction. Such documents are often filed for safekeeping with the solicitor who drew them. They are not released unless the grantor of the Power of Attorney requests it or his physician advises that the grantor is no longer capable. The person designated as attorney can then act in your interest.

"It's like having a whole town of next door neighbors. Everyone is so helpful."

- Penticton

"The young people are so pleasant."

- Penticton

"We moved from Vernon after a couple of years because, although we wanted to live in a small town, Vernon reminded us a lot of Sturgeon Lake and we did want something a little different.

"Originally, we moved to the Okanagan because this is where we honeymooned, so it has special memories for us. We'd never been to Penticton before since and then it was a boring little town. Unlike Vernon, though, it's changed in recent years."

- Harry and Norma

"It's difficult to say exactly why we like Penticton. It's small but not boring in the way that small towns can be. The people certainly are friendly, right from the first dayt we felt welcome. "What a change from Maple Ridge. We moved to Maple Ridge because we had a son in North Vancouver. He isn't there anymore, so there was no reason to stay."

- Chris and Anna

Penticton

In addition to that, Haven Hill Retirement Centre provides an intermediate care nursing home for 76 residents. You must be a B.C. resident for a year to get in. Trinity Centre is another intermediate care facility. Information about nursing homes and rest homes can be obtained from the Penticton Chamber of Commerce, 185 Lakeshore Drive, Pentiction, V2A 1B7.

Medical and dental services are on a par with the other valley communities.

Shopping

The downtown core area offers a wide variety of retail stores and services, including a very large Zeller's outlet, and there is a good supply of small neighborhood convenience stores.

Cherry Lane Shopping Centre houses the only Woodward's department store in the valley while Peach Tree Mall has Woolco. Cherry Lane is slightly smaller than the Kelowna mall but offers a wide variety of shops and services.

Recreation, Entertainment News, Radio and TV

Penticton has three golf courses, two of them 18-hole courses and the third a par-3 course. Green fees range from $6 per round for the par-3 to $18 for the semi-private Penticton Golf and Country Club.

Tennis courts are located near the beach areas of both lakes and there is a lawn bowling green in the city.

Penticton has one movie house with four cinemas in it. And an outdoor theatre operates in the summer. A museum and art gallery are located on Main Street.

A community recreation centre has programs for seniors and there is one seniors activity centre at the Pentiction Retirement Centre, 439 Winnipeg Street, Penticton, B.C., V2A 6P5. This centre has apartments for seniors and numerous social activities aimed to appeal to those over 55. In addition, the centre has 100 long term care beds.

The local newspaper is the Penticton Daily Herald. There are also a variety of throw-away advertising papers and Lower Mainland dailies are available by subscription. The Herald's address is 186 Nanaimo Avenue West, Penticton, V2A 1N4.

There are two local radio stations, CKOK and CKOR-FM as well as the CBC-FM and French services. Cable and pay television are available at the same rates as Kelowna.

"We didn't like Kelowna too well because it just seemed like a big city that had nothing to offer. . . . Penticton doesn't have the services that Kelowna does, but it's far more interesting. I suppose that it's the people that make it interesting."

- Retired Prairie farmer

Table A : Apartment Rental and Vacancy Rates in B.C.
   July 1986
   Source: Canada Mortgage and Housing Corporation
   86/06/06

	One Bedroom		Two Bedroom		Three/up Bedroom	
	Rent $	Vacancy %	Rent $	Vacancy %	Rent $	Vacancy %
Courtenay	301	4.1	349	8.9	311	2.3
Kelowna	334	1.0	394	2.3	394	2.8
Penticton	295	6.4	365	5.9	387	3.0
Vernon	308	8.7	356	7.3	363	10.2
Vancouver	429	0.6	571	1.4	656	2.3
Victoria	367	2.3	480	2.7	553	2.9

Table B: Monthly Home Rental Rates in B.C.
        Source: Royal LePage Survey of Canadian
        House Prices
        Based on Estimates of Fair Market Value

	Detached Bungalow	Standard Condominium
Burnaby	$800	$525
North Vancouver	$1,000	$525
Richmond	$850	$500
Surrey	$750	$550
Kerrisdale	$1,500	$950
West Vancouver	$1,050	$700
Kelowna	$500	$550
Penticton	$525	$375
Vernon	$550	$400
Victoria	$625	$500

Table C: Housing Prices in B.C. and Canadian cities
   July 1986
   Source: Royal LePage Survey of Canadian House Prices
   Based on estimate of fair market value

	Detached Bungalow	Standard Two-Storey	Standard Condominium
Lower Mainland			
Burnaby	116,000	135,000	58,000
North Vancouver	128,000	128,000	68,000
Richmond	125,000	125,000	73,000
Kerrisdale	210,000	165,000	145,000
West Vancouver	155,000		142,000
Kelowna	70,000		40,000
Penticton	68,000	40,000	
Vernon	63,000	54,000	38,000
Victoria	90,000	95,000	61,000
Calgary Woodlands	88,000	90,000	64,000
Saskatoon North and East	88,500	78,000	65,000
Winnipeg River Heights	89,000	61,000	60,000
Toronto South Etobicoke	125,000	125,000	60,000
Montreal Brossard St. Leonard Anjou	77,000	85,000	65,000
Halifax	129,000		110,000

Table D: Average Weekly Cost of Nutritious
Food Basket
June 1986
Based on price data collected by
Statistics Canada

	Family of 4	Couple in 60s
Victoria	105.00	50.46
Vancouver	102.22	49.11
Edmonton	104.86	50.73
Regina	91.94	44.17
Winnipeg	89.93	43.34
Toronto	105.80	50.70
Montreal	101.32	48.99
Halifax	90.34	43.63
St. John's	103.84	50.09

Table E: Climatic Indicators
Mean Daily Maximums, Mean Daily Minimums, Precipitation
Source: Canadian Climate Normals, 1951-80
Environment Canada
Temperatures in degrees Celsius, precipitation in mm

City	JANUARY			JULY			PRECIPITATION			
	Mean Daily Max.	Mean Daily	Mean Daily Min.	Mean Daily Max.	Mean Daily	Mean Daily Min.	Jan.	July	Year's Total	Days With Precip.
Penticton	-0.1	-2.7	-5.3	28.6	20.3	12.0	32.0	21.1	282.9	100
Kelowna	0.0	-3.3	-6.5	27.9	20.4	12.9	37.4	23.5	332.2	104
Vernon	-2.2	-4.8	-7.4	27.0	20.0	13.0	32.8	25.6	347.7	120
White Rock	5.3		-0.1	20.7		11.4	155.1	29.8	1092.8	156
Vancouver										
Harbor	5.1		1.2	21.9		13.3	217.8	42.7	1540.3	168
Airport	5.2		-0.2	21.9		12.6	153.8	32.0	1112.6	163
North Shore	5.3		0.2	22.7		12.7	256.6	57.1	1859.9	178
Victoria										
Airport	6.0		0.1	21.7		10.8	154.3	18.1	872.9	155
City	6.1	4.1	2.1	19.7	15.4	11.1	110.7	13.4	647.2	138
Parksville	4.7	1.6	-1.6	23.5	16.7	9.8	146.9	23.1	963.9	180
Comox	4.9	2.2	-0.6	22.7	17.4	12.1	193.2	27.8	1215.4	161
Saltspring Island	5.6		0.2	22.3		11.7	190.8	23.5	1065.2	149
Edmonton		-14.7			17.5				446.5	121
Regina		-17.3			18.9				397.9	114
Winnipeg		-18.3			19.7				535.2	121
Toronto		-4.4			21.8				789.9	134
Montreal		-8.9			21.6				999.0	164
Halifax		-3.2			18.3				1318.8	152

On housing

Cooperative Housing Federation of B.C.
4676 Main Street
Vancouver, B.C.
V5V 3R7
Information on housing coops.

B.C. Housing Management Commission
Suite 1701 - 4330 Kingsway
Burnaby, B.C.
V5G 1B2
Information about government-operated housing

B.C. Housing Foundation
198 West Hastings
Vancouver, B.C.
V6B 1G8

Shelter Aid for Elderly Renters
Ministry of Human Resources
Parliament Buildings
Victoria, B.C.
V8V 1X4

Victoria Real Estate Board
3035 Nanaimo Street
Victoria, B.C.
V8T 4W2

Vancouver Island Real Estate Board
Box 719
6374 Metral Drive
Nanaimo, B.C.
V9R 5M2
Information on the island except Victoria

Vancouver Real Estate Board
1101 West Broadway
Vancouver, B.C.
V6H 1G2

Fraser Valley Real Estate Board
Box 99
15463 - 104th Street
Surrey, B.C.
V3T 4W4
Information on White Rock
Okanagan Mainline Real Estate Board
1889 Stall Road
Kelowna, B.C.
V1Y 4R2

Demographics

Chambers of Commerce usually have up-to-date fact booklets on their particular community which detail the services available and profile the industry and the people of the area.

Victoria Chamber of Commerce
1020 Government Street
Victoria, B.C.
V8W 1X7

Parksville Chamber of Commerce
Box 99
153 Island Highway
Parksville, B.C.
V0R 2S0

Comox Valley Chamber of Commerce
2040 A Cliffe Avenue
Courtenay, B.C.
V9N 2L3

Kelowna Chamber of Commerce
544 Harvey Street
Kelowna, B.C.
V1Y 7N8

Vernon Chamber of Commerce
3700 Thirty-Third Street
Vernon, B.C.
V1T 5T6

Penticton Chamber of Commerce
185 Lakeshore Drive
Penticton, B.C.
V2A 1B7

Vancouver Board of Trade
500 - 1177 West Hastings
Vancouver, B.C.
V6E 2K3

White Rock Chamber of Commerce
15047 Marine Drive
White Rock, B.C.
V4B 1C5

Publications for Seniors

There are a number of publications available in British Columbia written specifically for people about to retire. Some are produced by government, others by organizations catering to seniors needs.

Citizen's Guide to Long Term Care in B.C.

Senior Citizens' Guide to Services in B.C.

Write to: Social Planning and Review Council
109 - 2182 West 12th Avenue
Vancouver, B.C. V6K 2N4

Retiring into Your Future

Write to: City Savings and Trust Company
777 Hornby Street
Vancouver, B.C. V6Z 1S4

Income Tax and Senior Citizens

Write to: Revenue Canada
1166 West Pender Street
Vancouver, B.C. V6E 3H8

Services for Senior Citizens in B.C.

Write to: 761 Cardero Street
Vancouver, B.C. V6G 2G3

Welfare Rights and GAIN

Wills and Estates

Write to: People's Law School
3466 West Broadway;
Vancouver, B.C. V6R 2B3

Community Resources for West End Seniors

Write to: J. Morton Foundation
969 Burrard Street
Vancouver, B.C. V6Z 1Y1

Newspapers

Greater Victoria

Times-Colonist
2621 Douglas Street
Victoria, B.C.
V8W 2N4

Oak Bay Star
202B - 2046 Oak Bay Avenue,
Victoria, B.C.
V8R 1E4

Esquimalt/Victoria Star
1620 A Government Street
Victoria, B.C.
V8W 1Z3

The Sidney Review
Box 2070
Sidney, B.C.
V8L 3S5

Greater Vancouver

Vancouver Sun/Province
2250 Granville Street
Vancouver, B.C.
V6H 3G2

Westender/Eastender
1035 Davie Street
Vancouver, B.C.
V6E 1M5

North Shore News
1139 Lonsdale Avenue
North Vancouver, B.C.
V7M 2H4

Surrey Leader
Box 276
Surrey, B.C.
V3T 4W8

North Delta Sentinel
10680 - 84th Avenue
Delta, B.C.
V4C 2L2

The Richmond News
118 - 3633 Third Avenue
Richmond, B.C.
V6X 2B9

Richmond Review
5811-A Cedarbridge Way
Richmond, B.C.
V6X 2A8

Delta Optimist
5020 48th Street
Delta, B.C.
V4K 3N5

White Rock

Peace Arch News
Box 131
1335 Johnston Road
White Rock, B.C.
V4B 4Z7

Kelowna

The Kelowna Courier
550 Doyle Avenue
Kelowna, B.C.
V1Y 7V1

Vernon

Vernon Daily News
3309 31st Avenue
Vernon, B.C.
V1T 1Z2

Penticton

Penticton Daily Herald
186 Nanaimo Avenue West
Penticton, B.C.
V2A 1N4

Courtenay

Comox District Free Press
Box 3039
1625 McPhee Avenue
Courtenay, B.C.
V9N 5N3

Parksville

Arrowsmith Star
114 East Hirst Avenue
Box 1300
Parksville, B.C.
V0R 2S0

Parksville-Qualicum News
Box 2579
Parksville, B.C.
V0R 2S0